THE DAY
I ALMOST QUIT

....AND OTHER STRETCHING EVENTS

Mike,

Fredのこの本を心から感謝して
お世話になったMikeにお贈り
します。

Camey
4/15/09

FREDERICK J. MOODY

Library of Congress Catalog Card Number: 97-92882

ISBN 978-1-57502-417-2

All scripture references are from
The New King James Version of the Holy Bible.

Printed in the USA by

*M*ORRIS
PUBLISHING

3212 E. Hwy 30
Kearney, NE 68847
800-650-7888

TO MR. BRUCE WARNER*

My elementary school principal,
a teacher,
a coach,
a friend,
a man God sent into my life
to show me what a man can be like.

You are one of the biggest reasons
that I did not quit.

Fred Moody

* "Borrowed Dad", Chapter 3

REACTIONS

"This book captures the reader by its warmth, humor, and honest description of God at work in everyday life. It seems that men are especially preoccupied by the challenges of the daily routine, the need to be strong and successful in occupation, family leadership, fatherhood, and marriage. And yet, whether by an unexpected serious crisis or the dullness of the daily job (or anything between), we find we are not really in control of our lives, not the decisive, strong, confident person we want to be, or that we think God wants us to be. Take heart! For it is in the every day "little miracles" and unplanned blessings that God drums through His message: "I love you, I am with you, I am working out my plan for you." In this book, the author uses anecdotes and vignettes from his own life to illustrate by example how God works, and how Christian faith matures. The result is a practical, comforting word of encouragement for life in this hectic, high-technology age."

Dick Desautel
Professor, Engineering
San Jose State University

"Drawing upon his life experiences, Dr. Fred Moody weaves his personal stories with powerful insights to illustrate the realities of Christian faith. In a sense, his entire life has been lived in preparation for this book — all of these diverse experiences have shaped his vitally important message of how God designs for our lives. The Day I Almost Quit is not an extended sermon, but a collection of richly textured tales that demand the respect of any thoughtful person, Christian or non-Christian alike. The book challenges you to think, to feel, and to question. If you have doubts about the Christian faith, read this book. If you want to learn about the life of a Christian, study the book. Once you pick it up, you will not be able to put it down. Join Dr. Moody as he explains, in the passage of time from youth to age, how buggy wheels, a track meet, a fencepost, butterflies, and even three gray-haired ladies can draw you to recognize God's participation in your life. If life is a journey with Him in control, enjoy the ride!"

Dr. Jonathan Hau
MBA, Ph.D
California State Cabinet Member, Gideons International
Chairman of Advisory Board of Salvation Army

"The Day I Almost Quit is a powerful document as well as a thrilling, entertaining and challenging story...one that so grabbed my attention that I was almost forced to read it in one sitting! It is the emotional, yet intelligent expression of the heart of a leading engineer with General Electric, with credentials that have brought him many honors and acclaim. Yet...his greatest joy is found in sharing his love for Jesus Christ and his family whether it be in a Rescue Mission in the heart of Silicon Valley or a committee or conference room in Washington, D.C., or in the ivory towers of a hi-tec corporation giant! I have watched his life and that of his wife and family for nearly a quarter century and have marveled at the consistency and humility he has shown in this demonstration of God's faithfulness and enabling grace and power in a life so yielded to Him. TO GOD BE THE GLORY! This, I believe is what Dr. Fred Moody and his dedicated wife desire even more than life itself. To anyone seeking God's best in their Christian life, even in the corporate world, I would recommend that The Day I Almost Quit be at the top of their reading agenda!"

Dr. Don B. Rood
Minister at Large
Western Director,
THE POCKET TESTAMENT LEAGUE, 1957 — 1986

"In this collection of anecdotes, Fred Moody has helped us to see God in a unique way. The accounts of God's workings in his personal life give us practical dimensions for trust and faith. When read as part of daily devotions, each anecdote can be an inspiration to *grow up into Him in all things.* I commend it to all who desire such growth."

Paul Yaggy
Aerospace Research Scientist — NASA
Director of Research, Development and Engineering,
  US Army Aviation System Command
Pastor
Mission Executive — OC (Overseas Crusade) International

CONTENTS

Introduction

Note: *Fictitious names have been given to some persons in order to protect the innocent (or 'guilty', depending on the viewpoint).*

INTRODUCTION

"I thought that at last I gave you something you could do--but I see I was wrong."

My self-confidence crashed and burned. The man who uttered those words was my technical leader. He was smart. People respected his opinions. He always had a stream of engineers coming into his office to ask questions. As much as I wanted to believe that he had made a mistake about my ability, I could not dismiss what he said. His brilliant reputation gave crushing validity to his opinion of me. I had never felt so discouraged. That day, I came close to walking away from one of the most enjoyable careers anyone could have wanted. It turned out to be one of the worst and best days I ever had. The worst thing was losing every bit of my self-confidence. The best thing was how God used this painful time in my life to do something unusual that not only made me glad, but also changed the direction of my career.

That was the day I almost quit. Many other days have come when I felt overly stretched, which led to discouragement because things looked impossible. There were days when I felt afraid, weak and overwhelmed, or days when I felt like a victim. I still have times when I feel stretched to the limit! But not for long. Whenever I begin to feel that way, my mind goes back to that dismal day early in my career, and I remember a statement in the Bible that I can use to confront any situation. It says,

...If God is for us, who can be against us? (Romans 8:31)

There are many other statements from the Bible scattered throughout this book that gave me strength, and a secure sense of purpose in the face of problems. You do not have to agree with my theology to recognize the feelings I had while passing through each problem. Whether you ever believed or even read the Bible, you can enjoy the lessons learned, the happy endings, and the turning points in my perspective that resulted. Since men have an inner compulsion to solve problems...to fix things...to make things better, we always are ready to hear what happened to someone else, and how it turned out. There is a lot of that in these pages.

Heart-to-heart talks early in my career helped me to realize that other men had feelings similar to mine: they got discouraged too, even though they rarely showed it. Regardless of job status, level of education, political opinions, or generational differences, I discovered that we have a common link when it comes to discouragement. *All of us have experienced it.*

Even on days when we feel the strongest...the most successful...and in control of our world...discouragement can come in a flash if we suddenly realize that our strength and resources are not enough to accomplish the demands placed on us. We can also make ourselves vulnerable to discouragement when we try to change something and make it better, whether it is our personal, family, professional, or career circumstances. That is because in order to change things, we may have to take a risk, or face uncertainty, or confront our weaknesses, or recognize the possibility of failure, or stand against the fear of losing. Just thinking about what might happen can bring on an attack of discouragement!

The worst thing about discouragement is that it can trap us in a pit of debilitation, demotivation, and despair! It can weaken us to the point of giving up... quitting... and turning our backs on challenges and responsibilities. Discouragement can bring crushing defeat and unhappiness to our own lives and to those we love the most.

I discovered a simple remedy for discouragement by listening to a lot of other men who were open enough to describe the feelings they had in various circumstances. Whenever I heard them telling about a struggle that brought discouragement, I felt an immediate kinship with them. Their feelings were my feelings. Their questions were my questions. Questions that had to be answered. Questions like,

"What do you do when...
...your son or daughter 'turns you off,' and you don't
   know how to fix things?" or..

"...you accidentally learn that the 'higher-ups' are
   blaming you behind closed doors for a business failure,
   in order to protect their own careers at the expense of
   yours?" or...

"...the greatest plan you ever dreamed of is blocked,
   and you have no power to fight back?" or...

"...you become the victim of an untreatable physical
   condition, which makes you feel alone and afraid?" or...

"...you unload your anger on someone else, saying
   things you wish you hadn't, but never can erase?" or...

"...your marriage is becoming a dead end of lifeless routine?"

I heard a lot of free advice in these discussions.

"Don't give up. You can do it."

"He'll get his. Just be patient. You can laugh at him some day!"

"Life is unfair. Don't rock the boat. No good deed goes unpunished!"

"Take care of yourself. Look out for number one!"

Much of this worldly wisdom was based on self-help and the assumption that somewhere inside we had the ability and power to solve any problem. But all too often, I only found an empty arsenal!

Some of the men who shared their pain also went on to describe how God worked to help them through the difficulty. They got my full attention, because I wanted to hear how God figured into the equation. Listening to their words, I found myself drawing strength, hope, and joyful anticipation in how God might work in my circumstances, too. This has been my motivation for writing this book.

The Day I Almost Quit is my response to the words of King David, who said about God,

> *I will tell of all Your marvelous works.*
> *(Psalm 9:1)*

My hope is that this book will encourage, challenge, and stimulate your faith. It is written for men who may be in the process of formal education, following a career path, working in a trade, and/or raising a family and establishing a home. These are the men I know best. I have been one of them! I am one of them now! And I believe that God gives the ultimate basis for overcoming discouragement, since He..

> *...Is able to do exceedingly abundantly above all that we ask or think, according to the power that works in us, (Ephesians 3:20).*

It is my prayer that as you read the chapters, you will be encouraged in every struggle you face because you find compelling evidence that God cares, and that His work exceeds our imaginations.

Fred J. Moody

EARLY YEARS

When I remember my early years, I feel an overwhelming sense of gratitude to God that He cared enough to send special people into my life to encourage me and give me direction.

F. J. M.

CHAPTER 1

BOARDS AND BUGGY WHEELS

I did not want to go to heaven! Not yet. My best friend in the fourth grade was Donald, and we were making a race car! Every morning after a bowl of Rice Crispies™ I ran to Donald's house a block away to start work again on the four-wheeled project. We sawed boards, pounded nails, and started over at least once a day with a better idea. I was the mastermind behind it, and every night I dreamed up a way to improve it. Donald was not mechanically inclined, and he thought all of my ideas were great! He couldn't pound nails straight, either.

I spent the month of June either in Donald's back yard, or squirming in a chair while his mother tried to scare me to death with the afternoon, mandatory, Bible lesson. It was torture! Not the lesson itself, but the anguish of being held hostage when we could have been building! I resolved that it must be the price you pay for having a friend with a fanatical mother. Donald and I both knew that the agony would last till she said "AMEN" at the end of a long prayer and released us. Other kids in the neighborhood knew her as "Mrs. Hellfire and Brimstone." That explains why they stayed away from Donald. I was his only friend, and I think that his mother's only mission at the time was to get me to heaven!

The Bible lessons were twisted a bit from the ordinary. She read about Noah's ark, Daniel in the lion's den, Samson knocking down the temple, and Joshua, whom I thought she said blew up the city of Jericho! But every lesson had a direct reference to me in it.

'Freddy, God's law says that you'll die and go to hell unless you repent of your sin and accept Jesus Christ as your personal Savior!" She would close her Bible and look directly at me. Then in a sugary voice, she would ask, "Wouldn't you rather go to heaven? God's law says you can be saved."

"I'd rather work on our race car just now."

I don't know if I had the guts to actually say that, or if I just thought it, but my lack of a proper response always ended the session. She would roll her eyes upward in their sockets with an exasperated sigh, tell us to bow our heads while she prayed, and then dismiss us to the back yard.

Donald's dad was like an obedient puppy. "Yes, dear. No, dear. Right away, dear." It did not matter what he was doing; if she called, he changed direction. Even when he was explaining how to solve difficult race car problems, we lost him instantly at the sound of her voice. But we needed his wisdom, so we suffered through the frequent interruptions.

He played a major role in our project by taking us to the store for orange crates, and he gave us nails from his tool shop. The hammer and saw were his. He found an old baby buggy and removed the wheels for us to use. The last big problem was making it turn corners. He drove us to the junk yard to get a real steering wheel off a wrecked car, and helped us hook it up with ropes and pulleys. It would not have passed quality control, because we had to turn it one full revolution before the front wheels responded, but it worked!

"We forgot to make a brake!" Donald said, as we stood back to admire our machine.

"We don't need a brake," I said, confidently. "I know how to stop it without a brake."

He got in and waited for me to start pushing. "We can drag one foot to make it stop."

"No," I said, with positive assurance. "I know how to make it stop without dragging your foot!" I began to push him to Cedar Street Hill several blocks away.

He believed what I said, and so did I! But I was not going to tell him the "secret" right away. Just in case he decided that the car was more his than mine, I wanted to be in a position to negotiate! He had already hinted that the car should stay at his house, and I wanted to keep it at mine.

My "secret" had the earmarks of ingenuity. It was the greatest idea I had ever had! No one else had ever thought of it. My logic went like this: I knew that when I pushed my sister in her wagon, I could stop it by pulling on the back instead of pushing. It worked on our race car, too. When Donald was in it for a test ride, I quit pushing and began pulling, and it stopped. I reasoned that the driver himself could pull back on the steering wheel and stop the car! I felt so smart! Gifted! Brilliant!

The floodgate of my brain was wide open now, and a new idea rushed into my head as I pushed Donald. "The car is moving because I am pushing it," I thought. "I could make it go forward if I were sitting in it and pushing on the steering wheel! Self propulsion! No engine needed!"

Finally we arrived at the top of Cedar Street hill, which ended at the Fox River boat launch. Even though I had pushed him all the way over, Donald wouldn't get out. He thought he should ride down the hill first, since the wheels and all the nails in the car were his. I thought I should go first because I knew how to make it stop.

We argued and I threatened to never tell him my secret of how to make the car move by itself, but he didn't care, so I let him have his way. He positioned himself at the top of the hill with one leg hanging over the side. I hoped that he would go into the river. The car began to roll and gain speed. Donald let out an excited squeal! He drove a straight line, and managed to stop it near the bottom of the hill by dragging his foot. He was bellowing about how much fun it was, but I tried to ignore his excitement.

He struggled to bring the car back up the hill. "Hurry up," I called. I wasn't going to help him. When I took my turn, I would apply my secret and stop it by pulling on the wheel. Then, I would push forward on the wheel, make a U-turn, and drive it up the hill without any help from anyone!

I stepped into the car and scooted my legs under the steering wheel. No leg hanging over the side for me! In seconds, I was rolling faster and faster down the hill! The speed of the pavement rushing by scared me. The buggy wheels clattered on bumps in the street, and the whole car was shaking. I was heading toward a weed patch. I spun the steering wheel around. It overcorrected! Now I was aimed at a row of concrete pillars. Donald was yelling something about stopping it, and I pulled back on the steering wheel so hard it almost came off! Faster! Out of control! Bash! Broadside into a pillar with a deafening crunch!

The next sound I heard was that of Donald running down the hill, yelling things at me, which would have compelled his mother to wash out his mouth with ammonia! The buggy wheels on one side were bent over, and I was still sitting on part of the wooden frame, holding on to the steering wheel.

We did not play together for weeks. The broken car laid abandoned in his driveway. Donald's mother had to put my salvation on hold.

Crashing the car did not bother me nearly as much as being unable to stop it by pulling on the steering wheel. I was not ready to admit that my idea was wrong. Not even to myself. There had to be some explanation.

There were other four wheeled projects. I could not make any of them stop or go by pulling or pushing on the steering wheel when I sat in them, and I did not know why. Finally in a high school physics class, I learned what was wrong with my ideas; they violated physical laws—laws that determined cause and effect long before I came along and tried to violate them!

That was a long time ago, but part of me still does not like to believe that I am wrong when I can't make one of my ideas work.

Today, I use physical laws to predict how things will behave. Sometimes it seems obvious, and I tell others what I think, based on intuition. Occasionally they "pour concrete," trusting what I said. When that happens, I get nervous. Then I hurry through an analysis to see if my intuition was correct. Sometimes I crash! Intuition can be wrong! I realize again that things do not happen based on what I think, but rather, they are governed by laws.

My crash in the race car happened because physical laws, rather than my "smart, gifted, brilliant" ideas, dictated the outcome.

The other laws that Donald's mother tried to push through my head were about life, death, and eternity. I am sure now that her flaming Bible lessons were not designed to keep us from having fun on those summer afternoons. Either she wanted Donald to have at least one playmate in heaven, or she did not want my life to be like that race car — downhill, out of control, destroyed. Maybe both. Someday I will thank her for spending so much effort on me. It was not in vain.

There is a way that seems right to a man,
but its end is the way of death. (Proverbs 14:12)

CHAPTER 2

CAPTIVATED BY A CARTOONIST

Donald's mom continued to tell me that I needed to accept Christ as my Savior, or I'd burn in hell forever. Not too tactful, but she probably had my best interest in mind. If I were to become a Christian, that would mean giving up movies and bad words, she told me; plus, I'd have to go to church willingly with them at least twice a week, and I was not ready for that! Donald would sit like the proverbial bump-on-a-log and listen to his mom's "hard sell" to me almost every time I went over to play. But I knew that she would give up after while and let us go outside. Besides, hell was a long way off.

She didn't give up easily, but kept trapping me into going to church.

"Can Donald play?"

"He can play when we come home from church."

"I'll come back later."

"Why don't you come with us?"

"I can't."

"I'll call your mother for permission."

My mother thought it was good for me to go to church. She usually said it was okay without consulting me first, and I would end up again with Donald's family on a hard wooden bench wishing I was someplace else. But there was one time when I really wanted to go with them to church. I would have begged to go.

Vaughan Shoemaker, once editorial cartoonist for two National newspapers, was going to give a talk at Donald's church, and draw cartoons! I never had heard of Vaughn Shoemaker before, but if he could draw, I wanted to see him! I loved to draw cartoons myself, and I was good at it; at least Mom said so. Everyone in my class came to me when they wanted something drawn. I thought that this would be worth seeing, so I arrived on my bike at Donald's house an hour before we had to get into the car and drive to church.

Someone introduced Vaughan Shoemaker. It made no difference to me that he had been the first to draw a religious editorial cartoon called, "Let's Put Christ Back into Christmas." The introducer said something about the artist winning a Pulitzer prize. I was swinging my legs on the front row, running out of patience! Finally, Mr. Shoemaker stood, and picked up a big piece of chalk. I can still remember how easily he made chalk strokes on a huge sheet of paper suddenly come alive with people, animals, and objects. Each picture told a story! I sat like a statue. "I want to draw like that someday," I thought.

The title of his talk was "God Guides My Hand." I don't remember much of it, except that he said he used to be poor at drawing, and had been kicked out of art school because he had no talent. He said that he had prayed to God about it. Then he had begun to read the Bible and had learned that Christ died and rose to forgive him and give him a new life.

Whatever he said that night impressed one elementary school kid who did not like sitting in church. I wanted Jesus to guide my hand, too. I listened as he said a lot of the same things Donald's mom had told me; but for the first time, I actually heard! This talk was coming from someone I admired instantly from the time he made the first chalk mark. He made an eternal mark on my life!

This single incident has encouraged me to pray that God would bring special messengers into the lives of family and friends to capture their attention, and help them hear what others may have tried to tell them.

One of my valued possessions is a large, original india ink editorial cartoon, which bears a penciled inscription at the bottom:

"To my dear brother in Christ, Fred Moody.
Vaughan Shoemaker."

It hangs on a wall in our family room. He gave it to me in appreciation for speaking about nuclear power to a group of his neighbors in a retirement community where he lived. This was 45 years after I heard him speak in Donald's church. I told him about the night I sat swinging my legs on the front row as he told what God had done in his life. Vaughan Shoemaker passed away a few years later.

Occasionally, I pause to study the drawing he gave me. Warm memories always come back. I am glad I had the opportunity to tell him, "Thanks, Vaughan. God used you in my childhood to help me hear His voice. What you said mattered because I wanted to be like you."

I will instruct you and teach you in the way you should go; I will guide you with My eye. (Psalm 32:8)

CHAPTER 3

BORROWED DAD

There was no warning. I was in the third grade when I rode to the store with my dad one evening. He said he was going away for a while. It was something about joining the Army engineers to build bridges in Alaska until World War II was over. A few days later, I turned and waved goodbye to him as he stood on the porch; then I turned the corner on my way to school. He would not be there when I came home, but he said he would be back in a couple of years. I would be the "man of the house" while he was gone and help Mom care for my baby sister, Joyce.

My dad wrote letters, sent Eskimo trinkets from Kodiak Island, and a check each month so that Mom could pay the bills. A midwest winter passed, and it was spring. Regular envelopes from Alaska stopped coming. One day Mom said we would be moving across town to live with Grandma, and I would be a fourth grader at a new school. That's where I met a man who helped me to overcome a painful problem, and encouraged me to dream big dreams for the future.

All the kids liked Mr. Warner, the principal. He played ball with the boys, twirled one end of a jump rope for the girls, and he knew us all by name. The teachers warmly referred to him as the "boss". Since he had recently been in the military, he taught us "Forward...march!" "Right face!" "Left face!" "About face!" "You can do it!" "At ease!" It was fun, but at times impossible, because some of us did not know right from left! Sometimes as he barked out commands, a wry smile came over his face. We knew what to expect as he quickened the pace, and we landed on top of each other in a giggling pile of arms and legs.

Mom took an accounting job at an automobile agency. One day she sat down between Joyce and me on the couch, put one arm around each of us, and said, "I don't think Dad is coming back."

"He'll be back!" I reassured her. "I know he will."

Joyce just hugged her Raggedy Anne doll.

It took another year before I seriously questioned if he was coming back. Sometimes I would hear Mom talking to her best friend, Winnie, on the phone when I was supposed to be asleep in bed. Another woman? What were they talking about? Mom cried a lot in those days.

A special delivery envelope came one day. Mom took it into a room and closed the door. She was crying again.

I clung to the hope that one day my dad would walk up the sidewalk to the front door and come home at last. Other kids talked about their dads and what kinds of jobs they had. I boasted, "My dad is with the Army engineers." Only a Christmas card came to me from Alaska that year. "He's doing secret work for the Army, and can't even write letters about it!" I lied, even though I almost believed it. Divorce was something you tried to hide in those days. If a parent died, it was easy to explain their absence. A divorce usually meant that you were defective.

But fourth grade went on. "Forward march!" "Right face!" "Left face!" "Hustle!" "You can do it!" We had begun to look like West Point Cadets! No more falling down! Mr. Warner smiled with pride. He had helped us to do the impossible! When I started fifth grade, I began to be afraid. I did not know what was wrong with me. No one else showed any signs of what I felt. Whenever I missed a day of school, I was afraid, almost to the point of tears, when 1 had to return. Christmas vacation ended, and my anxiety was so high that I was sick. It was like the first-day-of-school jitters, only a thousand times worse. I did not know why I was afraid. "Man of the house"? I was afraid even to walk out of the house!

The fear came and went at odd times. Today, they call it an "anxiety attack," and put you on medication. Back then, if castor oil did not cure you, they didn't know what to do.

My anxiety reached its limit one day in a social studies class. I don't know what triggered it, but suddenly my throat tightened and I began to cry. I tried to hide it by keeping my head down. The fuse was lit. I was choking back a gigantic sob. The kid across from me looked up from his book and asked, "What's the matter with you?" The library quietness of that classroom exploded with my uncontrollable sobs, and everybody was looking.

"Let's go outside." A gentle arm was around my shoulder, and the teacher led me out into the hall. I could not even speak because I was shaking so hard with sobs. Finally she took me to the principal's office to see "the boss".

I was still sobbing as I sat across the desk from Mr. Warner. It seemed that he was ignoring my condition, and he began to talk. He laughed as he told about his funny experiences in the army. I began to laugh between sobs. Finally, he said, "I think I know what you have." A grin came over his face. "It's called the 'blues.' It's when you feel like crying, and don't know why."

That was the most accurate diagnosis anyone could have made! I don't remember all he said, but whatever was wrong with me got better. The "blues" were gone when I left his office. "If you ever feel the 'blues' coming on again, come and see me."

There were several more episodes of the "blues" that ended in Mr. Warner's office. I always left with the feeling that I had been rescued. I did not realize the genius of his homespun therapy till years later, but it worked. He simply got me to talk about what I liked to do. Then he found a way for me to do it.

I liked to draw pictures and enjoyed reading comic books. "You know what this school needs," he said with a twinkle in his eye. "A comic strip! Why don't you draw one every week and put it up on the bulletin board outside the office?" Every week students and teachers gathered outside his office between classes to follow my continuing adventure strip of Raggs Rabbit.

I liked to show movies on my toy projector. "How would you like to operate the school projector?" I carried the 60 pound Bell and Howell sound projector down the steps every week and set it up in the gymnasium for the assembly, where I showed the series of ERPI classroom films.

I was clumsy at basketball. He coached me mornings before school started, and taught me how to dribble and shoot. I could run fast. He coached me in track, and he was more excited than I was the day I won four blue ribbons in one meet! He took me to watch my first Thanksgiving Day football game and drove me home at half time because I was shivering in the cold. He showed me how to swing a bat, and I hit the winning home run for our school team on several occasions.

If I got an exciting idea, I could hardly wait to tell Mr. Warner. One time, I wanted to get a flash camera and darkroom equipment to start a picture taking business. His enthusiasm was all I needed. "Forward, march!" "You can do it!" Later, I took the album pictures at several weddings and other special occasions, and even won a photo contest!

Eighth grade graduation finally arrived. It was a solemn ceremony with a flag salute, invocation, members of the school board, teachers, parents, relatives, and three rows of students on the stage, sitting at attention. Our home-room teacher called the name of each student, which was his or her signal to walk across the stage to receive a diploma and handshake from a smiling Mr. Warner. When my name was called, Mom bravely stood up with my flash camera aimed and ready. "Forward, march!" This was triumph! Then the handshake. He held me by the hand a moment longer. "If you ever need to borrow a dad, call me!" FLASH!

Borrow a dad? It turned out to be a great idea! I borrowed Mr. Warner for several father-and-son events during my high school years, but I remember the last one above all. It was Dad's night at one of the games during the football season. Dads of all the players sat on the sidelines with the team, each wearing the same number his son had on his jersey. "I'll be proud to wear your number!" he said when I called him. "I'm so glad you thought of me.

I don't remember if our team won or lost that night, but I remember the long talk Mr. Warner and I had, parked under the streetlight in front of Grandma's house. He asked about my plans. I told him that Mom wanted me to try college. Then he said something that I have cherished to this day: "Fred, you've got what it takes to become anything you want to be." He paused while it sank in. "You are a winner, if I ever saw one."

When I got out of his car to go into the house, he reached out and shook my hand one last time, curling my fingers around some rolled up dollar bills. The last thing he said before driving away was, "Remember, you can do it!"

I stood on the porch as the red tail lights of his car went out of sight. That was the last time I saw him, since I went off to college the next year. A second year of college passed, and I was married. There was no more need for me to borrow a dad.

Mr. Warner was an elementary school principal by position, but also a special man God sent into my life to be there when I needed a dad, a counselor, a coach, a friend, and a man to help me see what a man can be. His words are still vivid. "You can do it!" "Forward, march!"

A father of the fatherless, a defender of widows,
is God in His holy habitation. (Psalm 68:5)

CHAPTER 4

THE PHONE CALL

This was going to be my best year. I could feel it. The graduating varsity football players at our high school traditionally elected next season's captain from the upcoming junior class. The coach announced at the end-of-the-season football banquet that I had been chosen! Sudden status was mine! The whole school knew who the captain was. Hopes and dreams began to form in my mind from that day, and my anticipation increased through the winter, spring, and summer that followed. Winning games! Friday night victory parties! A championship? Then it was fall and football season started again.

Practice. Morning and afternoon. Falling into bed early. Running, tackling, catching, grunting, groaning, sweating, a bad case of sore muscles, and repeat. The first game was several weeks away.

Our practice schedule was interrupted by the start of school, and a new girl named Rhonda. She was the hot topic of hallway discussion among the guys. Short, flirty, and from Chicago. Different from the small town girls we knew. She smoked cigarettes and carried a big purse on a shoulder strap. None of the other girls had progressed to that level of womanhood! I don't remember how we met, but as soon as she found out I was the football captain, she invited me for a Sunday afternoon visit. She had come to live with her aunt and uncle for a while—something about not getting along with her mother. Most of my low-flying crowd listened to singers like Rosemary Clooney, and Les Paul and Mary Ford. Rhonda was high-flying, enthralled by Edith Piaf, Ertha Kitt, and classical music.

The guys at school considered us a "serious couple" after two or three afternoon visits. That was okay with me. After all, this was my best year! Being captain seemed to put the freeze on any other guy showing a dating interest in her. I was immune from competition.

Rhonda's aunt and uncle lived in the same house where a classmate named Sherwood used to live. Sherwood was not athletic. He was more of a politician-president of the debate team, a senior class officer, and other brainy activities. One day Rhonda told me, "I can't believe it! That person! Sherwood! Or whatever his name is. He said that he and I would get to know each other better when he took me out on a date. As if I would even consider it! Such arrogance I never knew existed!"

"No competition," I assured myself, thinking that I completely understood women. Sherwood was a bore! Girls would rather go with the high-visibility stars on the football team!

Our first game was played on a hot, sticky midwestern Saturday afternoon. Each school band played, trying to outdo the other. The cheerleaders yelled till they were hoarse. Students filled the bleachers. I spotted Rhonda in the crowd shortly after our team made a grand entrance onto the field.

The only thing that went right on the field that day was when I led the team warmup calisthenics. We looked sharp, and sounded unbeatable as we did jumping jacks while thundering, "One-two-three-four!" in unison. Things began to deteriorate after the opening kickoff. Whatever happened between the kickoff and final gun, no one could say for sure, except that we lost. We went to the bus in shock. Rhonda consoled me. The rest of the season would be better. One loss did not change the fact that I was captain. It was the team that lost. My status did not change, I thought.

A new development occurred. It was a terrible thing! It wasn't that we lost all of our games that year except one. The terrible thing was that the coach did not let me start any of the remaining games. It was like he held me personally responsible for our first loss! I went out at the start of each game to meet the other captain, stood there for the coin toss, and then returned to the bench with all the second stringers.

Up until then, whoever was the captain had retained a sure place on the first string team. But now the coach put Hal in my place! I could have understood it if Hal were an outstanding player, but he wasn't. The rest of the team wanted me to play. I gained yards. Hal lost. I could run fast. Hal was slow. It did not matter how well I performed in practice. The games started with me on the bench, and sometimes I hardly got to play at all. My frustration was unbearable. I made several trips to the coach's house to ask why. He said that I did better in practice, but Hal did better in the games. How could he say that when I was on the bench most of the time? Later I consoled myself in a rumor

I'd heard. Hal's dad was a contractor, who at that time was remodeling the coach's house at dirt cheap cost. I had to be a victim of politics!

Then an even worse thing happened. I learned that a captain, if he sits on the bench, can lose his status. Rhonda became less interested in me. I was hoping that she would ask me to the annual girls-ask-guys Christmas Dance. It was a plush affair with formals and rented tuxedos. But time was passing and she didn't mention it. No phone call. She was cool toward me in the halls. And one day—DEVASTATION. I learned that Rhonda had asked Sherwood! Sherwood, the wimp! The sissy! The smooth talking, arrogant one she said she would never date! I found out his secret! He had impressed her by promising to bring along two bottles of champagne! I was sick. My dreams of a best year had died.

I was at home alone on a cold, gloomy Saturday, wondering if I would be able to forget my pain in 10 or 20 years. It would have been nice to go to the dance. But who wants a forgotten captain? A disgrace? A nobody?

The phone rang. "Probably for Grandma," I muttered. We were living with her. "She's the only one who gets calls around here."

I did not recognize the girl's voice. "Is this Fred Moody? You don't know me. I'm Phyllis Ivemeyer. If you have no other plans, I would like to invite you to the Christmas Dance."

I thought all the dates had been made. Every girl had picked her escort by now. Because of this angelic voice at the other end, I was beginning to feel a little like somebody again. "Uh...when is it?" I knew when it was. I said I might be going out of town, but I would call her back. I had no travel plans to anywhere, but I did not want to appear anxious.

After we hung up, I hurried to find the yearbook to see who she was. I stood by the window studying her junior year picture for a long time. Nice smile. Pretty eyes. How come I'd never met her before? I called her right back.

The Christmas Dance was alive with the smell of winter corsages. Rhonda was there with Sherwood. She was already tipsy, and excused herself periodically for a smoke. I did not realize it then, but the unpretentious, genuinely sweet girl doing the two-step with me was a gift from God!

A week or so after the dance came a quiet New Year's eve with Phyllis in front of her black and white TV. A week later, it was her

14

birthday. I bought her a necklace. We began to go to a lot of events together. It did not matter to her that I had been the captain who ended up on the bench. She liked me anyway. Neither one of us practiced much religion at the time, but we decided that God must have given us to each other so that we could become something together. Two years later, we were married.

Sometimes I have a chilling thought. What if our team had won our games? What if I had been the hero I wanted to be? I might have missed the most important phone call of my life.

He has made everything beautiful in its time.
(Ecclesiastes 3:11)

CHAPTER 5

MY LAST TRACK MEET

I was on the varsity track team. It was a blustery day in May with intermittent sun, clouds, rain, and cold wind. West High was competing with seven other schools in the final Big Eight outdoor track meet of the year. I was too slow for the sprints, too low on endurance for long distance, and too clumsy for hurdles, broad jump, high jump, or the pole vault. My hope for glory that year was the quarter mile dash. That's once around the track as fast as you can go. I was the fastest in our school. I worked hard all year to be good enough to win. Sprinting, torturing myself, getting to bed early. Cutting out candy, ice cream, and malteds. I would run until I couldn't run any more, and then I'd make myself go for another lap.

But all the pain seemed to be wasted. I kept losing! My best time at the end of the season was only five seconds better than it had been at the beginning. The last hundred yards of every race always felt like it was happening in slow motion with excruciating aches in my arms and legs, which got heavier with each step.

I dreaded this particular day. I knew that I would be running against guys from other schools who had beat me in previous track meets that season. I usually was third or fourth to cross the finish line. Seven schools at the same time? How could I even place? I felt sick.

I prayed. It wasn't based on deep theology, and I was not sure that God heard it, but I was desperate. I hoped God might cause the other runners to trip, get sick, eat a big lunch and get cramps, or be scholastically ineligible. Maybe I would be the only person at the starting blocks if He could work it out!

It didn't happen that way. They all showed up. I recognized them from the back, because that was what I had watched as I was chasing them in the other meets.

We ran the race in several groups because there were so many runners. I ended up in a group of who had all come in ahead of me before. I wanted to go home! The judges would time everyone individually, and list the times in order after all the groups ran.

"To your marks!" Long nervous pause. "Set!" A tense breathless moment. "Bang!" And we were pounding down the cinder track in a stampede to get out in front early.

We reached the quarter point, and I had managed to stay in the cluster of runners. It was always the second half when they sped up and I slowed down. If I could just outrun one person, I would not come in last!

The sun had disappeared behind a cloud, and as we moved out of the quarter point to the opposite side of the track, we were heading into a high, gusting wind! Sounds of shoes hitting the cinders, along with grunts, bellows, and gasps for deeper breaths were all but drowned out by the wind blowing. I suddenly realized that I could not feel the wind! Other runners shoulder-to-shoulder ahead of me formed a moving wall which shielded me!

As the race continued to the three-quarters point, I was like a sports car following close behind a semi-truck on the highway, being sucked along in its wake! They were slowing down, and so did I. They were giving all they had; I was resting. When we came to the home stretch, the wind was at our backs. Those who made the moving wall for me were out of kick, and I felt like I was just starting! I passed them and won! The wind kept blowing, and no one else's time was better than mine! A blue ribbon! My time was slow, as usual, but it was faster than anyone else's on that day!

Today when I have to face what looks like an impossibility for me, I remember that track meet. God gave me a hint of His sovereignty that day, when He showed me that He can arrange events, including the weather, to make the impossible become possible. I think that He gave me that experience to convince me that "..I can do all things through Christ who strengthens me." (Philippians. 4:13)

The race is not to the swift, Nor the battle to the strong, Nor bread to the wise, Nor riches to men of understanding, Nor favor to men of skill; But time and chance happen to them all.
(Ecclesiastes 9:11)

BITS AND PIECES

God sent some faith-stretching experiences into my early adult years, which helped me to look for His marvelous working in everyday events.

F. J. M.

CHAPTER 6

NO WAY TO CONVINCE THEM

It was my second semester at Blackburn, a liberal arts college in southern Illinois, where the students worked 20 hours a week to operate the school and keep their tuition costs down. My first semester had been a good one. I managed to get one of the few A's given in analytic geometry, taught by Professor Bretthauer. He loved students and the subject alike. He taught with conviction, emotion, and a passion to brand the theorems, proofs, and oddities into our brains so deeply that we would whisper them with our dying breaths! We could hardly wait for his class each day so we could watch him unfold the mysteries of mathematics. His kind of teaching was rare.

Chemistry class was the opposite. The subject was okay, and I was eager to learn about chemical reactions, if for no other reason, to learn why fireworks did what they did so that I could invent some new ones someday. (Fireworks had been a hobby of mine since sixth grade.) But Professor Stall had less personality than a fungus growing in the grass. I remember him standing tall and slender in front of the class, almost motionless for an hour, droning on in a lull-you-to-sleep monotone. He looked like a figure you'd see in a wax museum, except that his eyes blinked occasionally behind thick glasses, and his mouth, with traces of lunch residing in the corners, appeared to move in synchronization with his words. No emotion. No crescendos. No speeding up or slowing down. Just words.

I had learned to stare at him with an interested expression while I daydreamed. He was just a head on a body, making sentences so long that I would forget where he started by the time he got to wherever he was going. We studied the chemistry book during the week and had a quiz every Saturday morning.

As soon as classes were over each Friday, I would walk away from the campus, taking a different route each time. When I was sure that no one had followed me, I would turn down the street to a dilapidated garage I was renting for five dollars a month from a widow, and pick up my 1940 Chevy. It was against the rules for freshmen to have cars, but my situation was different.

Phyllis was 60 miles away at Illinois State College in Jacksonville.

One such Friday afternoon, I sat in chemistry class, my thoughts already on the road to Jacksonville. The class was disorderly because there was a homecoming event that evening with a bonfire, food, and a dance. It was to be a chaperoned mixer for guys and girls from both dorms. Anticipation among the guys was unusually high, although I did not know why. Most of the girls at Blackburn were from southern Illinois farms. Their idea of a fun date involved going down to the barn to watch the new milking machine! But this afternoon, everyone around me was talking, passing notes, laughing, and not paying attention to Professor Stall. It was like the class was purposely trying to get him to lose his temper. Nothing happened. His mouth continued to move.

Then came a surprise. No one expected it. Three minutes were left and, although he always mumbled up to the bell, the droning stopped abruptly. The classroom undercurrent tapered to dead silence. Then his mouth opened. "Since the class has had more to say than I have today..." His words were slow and carefully chosen... "You obviously have learned everything that will be on the quiz tomorrow morning. Being such a brilliant class, you will not object to leaving your books in your rooms. It will be a closed book quiz. I caution you, however, that you will need to know the valences in Table 5 of Chapter 7 in order to answer the questions."

We sat motionless as he walked down the center aisle and left the room. Silence. Then someone said, "If he thinks that I'm going to take my chemistry book on a date tonight and memorize that table, he's nuts."

Others affirmed. Back at the dorm, guys already were working on ways to overcome this obstacle. Some wrote the table on the inside of their shoes, on partly shaved ankles, or on their stomachs.

I thought, "This is unreasonable! No one could work any test without Table 5. Everyone else has a system, so why should I be different?" My system was a small card, taped to the inside of my left wrist where it would not show with my shirt sleeve buttoned.

I went to see Phyllis, and got back from Jacksonville late that night. The alarm clock woke me Saturday morning, and I got my equipment together before going to the quiz. Soon, we were all in our places. There was an atmosphere of "We'll show you!" A few girls with higher standards had tried to memorize the table, but it was too much. Each had resigned herself to getting a failing grade on this one quiz, rather than face the wrath of God for something as bad as—a card taped to the wrist!

Professor Stall arrived with an upperclass woman assistant, who began to hand out the quizzes. I assumed from her steady frown and business-like stomping from row to row that she had missed out on a date the night before. My sleeve was unbuttoned, but still hanging down to cover the illegal card. "You may start," she said.

Professor Stall had taken a seat behind the desk, and was peering at the class. I could see students casually loosening their shoes, or sliding their socks down, or lifting their shirts to get a view of their stomachs. It was disgusting, but necessary.

I thought, "I've never done anything like this! He may be dull, but he's not dumb! He will know that we cheated." I felt a triumphant resolve coming over me. "I got an honest A in analytic geometry! An honest F on a chemistry quiz would be better than a dishonest A ." I began to button my sleeve. The button didn't want to go through the buttonhole.

"May I see what you have there?"

I froze! It was her! Somehow she had drifted from the front of the classroom to my desk in the back without a sound! She was pointing to my almost buttoned sleeve. I searched her face for a hint of understanding. Instead, her cold expression was like that of an executioner. She tore off the card with the tape and a swatch of hair, and snatched up my blank quiz paper. Then she whirled around, strutted up the aisle, and plopped the evidence onto the desk in front of Mr. Stall. She bent down to whisper something in his ear, pointing at me several times. He whispered back. I felt like a sacrificial lamb—innocent, but slaughtered anyway! Others around me had panicked, and were quickly pulling up their socks, or tucking in their shirts, and trying to look hard at work.

No one would believe me if I said that I was trying not to cheat. The evidence could never show what my true intention was. I shuffled up to the desk after the quiz. An F grade on one quiz was the least of my concerns. The thing that mattered most at that time was what Professor Stall and his assistant were thinking about me.

"No one does that in my class," he said in his characteristic monotone. I tried to say something, but he walked away, and his assistant followed.

I walked. Probably many blocks. This should have been a happy time, because shortly I would get my car and drive to Jacksonville again to see Phyllis. But my thoughts were in a swirl. I had to think this through. Guilty to others. But really innocent. A victim. No way to fight. Condemned.

I did not notice the car that had slowed and was keeping pace with me. "Young man! Get in. I'll give you a lift!" An older gentleman with short, grey hair and a smile reached to open the door. I got in. "You look like you lost your last friend! Bad news or something?"

My troubles came pouring out and he smiled, knowingly. "Just remember, 'This above all: to thine own self be true.' That comes from Shakespeare."

I concluded he must be an angel from heaven to help me get through this. It did seem unusual that an angel would utter a quote from Hamlet! But maybe so. Anyway, I began to feel the heaviness lift, and soon I was ready to drive to Jacksonville.

The following week I was called into the Dean's office. "We decided to give you a second chance. But you should know that we were ready to put you on a train and send you home."

I mumbled something in a repentant voice like, "It won't happen again. Thank you for giving me another chance."

I doubted his remarks about sending me home on a train. It was obvious that the school needed all the students and tuition money they could get. The next thing he said made the whole incident take on a deeper significance.

"The reason we decided to let you stay is that someone on our staff interceded for you. He believes in you. He thinks that you have what it takes. Mr. Bretthauer went to bat for you, and he's waiting to see you in his office now."

Mr. Bretthauer? A second angel? Two angels in one week? One who quotes Shakespeare, and one who teaches math?

I know they were not angels, but I am thankful to God for sending them both.

He chose us in Him (Christ) before the foundation
of the world, that we should be holy
and without blame before Him in love.
(Ephesians 1:4)

CHAPTER 7

A QUESTION OF LIFE AND DEATH

We were husband and wife now. It had been the happiest two weeks of our lives. Phyllis sat on the front seat beside me, her brown hair blowing as she watched Nebraska farmland passing by. It was her and me forever.

My 1940 Chevy bulged with everything we owned, including Phyllis' dusty Bible in one of the boxes, for good luck. Our great adventure would begin in Boulder, Colorado, where she would work and I would finish school at the University. Our happiness could not be diminished by the constant engine overheating, which forced us to add water at every gas station.

We moved into our first apartment on a back alley parallel to University Avenue. When we opened the door, a welcoming committee of cockroaches sped in every direction. The ugly, soft-shelled beasts were the landlady's pets, thriving on the venison she always forgot to put away. We held them at bay on her side of the house by sprinkling a heavy strip of lethal blue powder across the threshold of the bathroom, which we shared with her (and them)!

It was a ten minute walk to the campus. I enrolled in the engineering school, and Phyllis found a clerical job in the records office so we could pay our bills. She could retire when I graduated, and then we would step up to the "professional class" where smart, rich, and exciting people lived. We were not in a hurry because we were happy.

We made many friends who also were submerged in college life. Lots of activity. Lofty plans. A mission in life. Going someplace. Full of expectations. The professional way! We began to get a taste of it long before I graduated. It was a preview of our future! Both of us had come from working class families, but the professionals seemed to have it all!

Mr. Swank was my idea of a successful man. He was financially independent, but kept active in new business ventures "just to have fun," as he described it. We met the Swanks at church. They were a happy, warm, middle aged couple. They also had a beautiful home with manicured grounds, expensive cars, a garage bigger than our whole apartment, a curved driveway, marble entry way, thick carpets, elegant furniture, and picture windows looking toward the Rockies! One day, this would be us! No more alley doors. No old car that overheated. No cockroaches, or bathroom to share.

One evening I jumped up from a chair to show Phyllis the newspaper. The first sentence gave the main details:

RETIRED MANUFACTURER DIES

Mr. B. Swank, active member of the Rotary Club, the Lion's Club, the Optimists Club, and the Country Club, fell dead on the kitchen floor after raiding the refrigerator, still clutching a turkey sandwich, leaving a wife, and grown children Rich, Randy, and Rebeccah.

It went on to discuss his many achievements, and gave details about the funeral service, which must have had all the pomp of a hero's sendoff!

"This should not have happened," I thought. "Not to a man who enjoyed life like he did! It's unfair! He's dead!" This was something I tried to forget quickly.

I spent most weekends studying, so on most Sunday afternoons, Phyllis and I were ready to take a walk. Sometimes we strolled holding hands in Pioneer Park, a half block from our apartment. Gravel paths, pine trees, soft breezes. But tombstones everywhere, marring the otherwise beautiful surroundings! It was a place I enjoyed and hated at the same time. The thing I enjoyed was that we were together in something like a garden. But I hated the reminder of our temporariness as we read grave stones. You could find every kind of stone in Pioneer Park. There were home made stones of mortar poured into a shoebox, engraved with a blunt stick. Some monuments stood ten feet tall, testifying to the wealth or success of someone buried underneath who couldn't even enjoy the gawking admiration of onlookers. Mr. Swank was buried somewhere else, and I expect that his monument rivals the *arc de Triomphe!*

It troubled me that no matter how much success you achieve, it does not change the fact that life as we know it here is temporary, and each of us will eventually end up under a stone with our name on it.

About that time, a question rose to the surface of my mind, causing me to feel that I could never fully enjoy life unless it was answered. My question was basic, but the only people that seemed to care were the bereaved at funerals:

WHAT HAPPENS WHEN YOU DIE?

> Do you go somewhere else; or does the light just go out, your thoughts stop, and you cease to exist?

I had collected a few opinions from people, who were enjoying life to the fullest. I thought for sure that they would have some answers. I was disappointed at what they said.

Mr. J. (successful engineer): "Is oblivion impossible to face? I think when you're dead, it's all over. Garbage. Nothing more." (That sounded like a self-image problem to me.)

Mr. R. (marketing person, who knew how to close a deal): "I was unconscious for several days after an accident. During that time, I had no conscious thought- just a black void. You cease to exist when you die." (If that is true, I cease to exist every night until the alarm goes off! When you don't exist, do you still snore?)

At least two people had a flicker of hope for immortality:

Mr. G. (shrewd businessman): "I suppose if there is a heaven, that's where I'll go. I really haven't given it much thought."

Mrs. D. (next door neighbor, and social butterfly): "I believe in life after death. I've told my children to bury me under a rose bush so that I can be reborn as a beautiful rose!" (She wanted to be fertilizer!)

I decided that personal beliefs about death were as diverse as fingerprints–no two exactly alike, and of significance only to the ones who claimed them.

"Religion must have the answer," I thought, so we joined a church. We wondered if we should unpack Phyllis' Bible, but since no one else brought one, it stayed in the box. We were welcomed into the fellowship with handshakes and warm greetings.

A knock sounded on our alley door the next evening. An older gentleman had come from the church to discuss membership. He had a gentle smile, understanding eyes, and wrinkles that betrayed years of experience and wisdom. After one look at him, I believed that my question would be answered before he left our apartment.

He sat at the table and took a printed card out of his coat. He wanted general information about us for church records. We gave him our full names, address, and phone number as he dutifully wrote, licking the point of his pencil between words.

He paused at the next line, looked up and asked, "How much will you give every week?"

"What?"

He cleared his throat, and asked again. Then he looked back and forth at both of us with that gentle smile, and waited.

I could not comprehend the absurdity of that moment! I felt my neck get warm, but I was determined not to be one who spoke next. Even though Phyllis looked at me for some response, my silence outlasted our visitor's. He laid his pencil on the card. "I'll wait here if you both want to go into the other room and discuss it." We decided on twenty-five cents per week, just to get rid of him.

My question got buried under a heavy load of end-of-the-semester tests. One Sunday night, Phyllis had gone to bed, and I was studying late for a big test scheduled for the next day. At that particular time in my life, I had structured a prayer to use on occasions where I faced something important. It went like this: "Dear God, help!" Then, I would supply enough details so He knew what kind of help to give. That night, I asked Him to help me on the test.

I was still sitting at my desk in the corner of the living room with only a study lamp on. The rest of the apartment was dark. I was tired, and my mind began to wander away from the open book in front of me. I should have been happy, but I was distressed. A job offer was coming in the mail from the General Electric Company in California. Our dreams were about to come true, but it troubled me because I had seen that dreams can be interrupted with cruel suddenness—like Mr. Swank, dropping dead on the kitchen floor.

I realized that my structured prayer was pitifully lacking. I had to call out, and for the first time I can remember, I told Him how I felt inside. "God, don't go away yet. I should be happy, but I'm not. I'm afraid. Our dreams could be cut off, just like Mr. Swank. I need some answers. What about dying?" I did not know how else to ask, but God understood, as He showed me in the weeks that followed.

The next day came, and I passed the test.

The job offer arrived. I accepted.

We drove to California in February, avoiding icy roads by taking the southern route. We moved into a new apartment without cockroaches! I started to work as an engineer.

One of the first friends I made was a veteran engineer, who invited us to visit his church. Since I did not want to offend him, we went. Everyone at his church carried a Bible, even little kids who couldn't read!

The choir had saved their best anthem until just before the offering-obviously to get people in a good mood to give money. Then the minister stepped to the podium to address the audience. That reminded me of the older gentleman who had come to our apartment, asking, "How much can you give every week?" I was sitting next to my friend, who reached for his wallet, and I began to fumble for mine so I would not look cheap. I expected to hear a whining plea for funds. It didn't happen like that.

"We do not want you to give anything to this offering," said the minister, "unless you know Christ. This offering is for those who have trusted in Him as their Savior. If you haven't done that yet, we want you to give yourselves to Him."

The next Sunday came and I wanted to go back to the same church. We kept going every week. We unpacked Phyllis' Bible after the first Sunday, and I began to get up every morning to read it with the excitement of a blind man who could see for the first time. I made a lot of notes because I felt that I had to capture and keep the precious moments of revelation that flowed from its pages. I was finding answers to my question about death, plus answers to other questions that I had not even thought to ask. The answers were there all the time in an unopened box!

Now I know in part, but then I shall know
just as I also am known.
(I Corinthians 13:12)

Epilogue to Chapter 7

"What happens when you die?" leads to other questions, like, "Who really knows the truth?"

The best person to answer any question is one whose truthfulness and credibility are validated. If we want to know what's going to happen when we face an operation, it is best to ask the surgeon. If we want to know what happens when we die, it is best to ask one who has seen the other side of death. This leads to another important question. "Where do you find someone who has died, that can tell you by experience what happens?"

Some people report near-death experiences, where their vital signs stopped, and they were pronounced clinically dead. They describe seeing a tunnel of light, or hovering above those trying to revive them. Other accounts describe intense sorrow and distress. The multitude of these threshold experiences, taken together, raise more questions than they answer, and abound with confusion, based on what I observe. I concluded that the range of experiences is much like the range of opinions people have about death--misleading and inconclusive.

Statements I found in the Bible point to Jesus Christ as the only person who can speak with authority and credibility about death. Since I was serious about wanting a truthful answer, it made sense to search for whatever He had said about death, because many have believed for centuries that He died and rose again from the dead.

Christ said in the famous Sermon on the Mount that death is a transition, not a sudden void:

> *Enter by the narrow gate; for wide is the gate and broad is the way that leads to destruction, and many there are who go in by it. Because narrow is the gate and difficult is the way which leads to life, and there are few who find it, (Matthew 7:13, 14).*

I think that if it were our responsibility, we could not find the narrow gate that leads to life! But it is not hidden from anyone who calls on God to *show* him where it is:

> *Whoever calls upon the name of the Lord shall be saved.*
> *(Romans 10:13)*

The Bible says that the narrow gate is a Person, not a path:

> *Jesus said..."I am the way, the truth, and the life. No one comes to the Father (God) except through Me." (John 14:6).*
> *I am the door. If anyone enters by Me, he will be saved...*
> *(John 10:9).*

The Bible also says that when someone dies who has asked God to show him the "narrow gate", his soul leaves his body behind and passes immediately into heaven:

> *We are confident, yes, well pleased rather to be absent from the body and to be present with the Lord.*
> *(II Corinthians 5:8).*

Christ stood before the tomb a dead friend's relatives had just opened. Before He called the dead man back to life, He said:

> *I am the resurrection and the life. He who believes in Me, though he may die, shall live. And whoever lives and believes in Me shall never die... (John 11:25, 26).*

This was a new insight on death for me. It implies that when death occurs to those who believe in Christ, they close their eyes on this life, and, in a twinkling, open them in His presence without interrupting life.

I know that I do not have the full answers to my questions, but I am still learning. Like everyone else, my view is limited. My eyes only capture the visible spectrum, but there is a vast range of electromagnetic waves I cannot see. My ears can only hear a limited frequency range, not even as much as a dog! My thoughts can only comprehend up to a limit (the terms "always existed" and "everlasting" do not register in my mind). But the answers I find in the Bible about death, and about life, are all that I need now. I can be content just to know that He, whom I have trusted, is the Gate that leads to life.

> *God so loved the world that He gave His only begotten Son, that whosoever believes in Him should not perish but have everlasting life.*
> *(John 3:16).*

CHAPTER 8

CONFLICT OF INTEREST

My dad left our family when I was in the third grade, and that caused big problems for me. Today, they would say that I had an identity problem. It's funny when I remember ways I tried to compensate. I made fireworks and bombs out of tin cans and chemicals you could get at the drug store! I could have been killed when one blew up as I was attaching a fuse in our basement. The scorched hair and hundreds of blisters on my arm made me a hero to my friends!

When I outgrew my childhood, adolescent and teenage years, I thought I also outgrew my identity problem. I was married and going to college in Boulder, Colorado, but I still had a compulsion to prove to others that I was somebody! I was finally set free from the compulsion one snowy morning in February. We were asleep.....

"Phone call for Fred!" Our landlady was banging on the wall of the bathroom that joined our apartment with hers. We had to share her phone, too, since we could not afford one of our own. The ring was wired to a bell, and it sounded like a fire alarm because Mrs. Stuart was hard of hearing.

"Coming!" I called as I nearly fell out of bed, and scrambled to find my slippers. I would never walk through Mrs. Stuart's apartment again with bare feet! Her floor was a haven for assorted crawling things that crunched or squished under my feet. Phyllis had given me a pair of slippers for Christmas. I knew that she had given me two, but so far I had only found one under the bed. By now, Phyllis was sitting up, adjusting her pincurls and blinking as she tried to make sense out of my scurrying around.

The phone call had to be from the Microswitch Company in Denver, where I had applied for a job. They had advertised an opening for a technician with fairly high pay. It did not require a college degree. Their ad had appeared several times in the paper. Each time I saw it, I grew more dissatisfied with our frugal existence! Our social life had sunk to the excitement level of a convalescent hospital. A Saturday night movie at the Flatiron Theater was the poverty-level highlight of our week! Or we could have pizza if we skipped the movie! I was ready for a step up--a newer automobile, an occasional drive to Denver for dinner at an expensive restaurant, shopping, and performing arts whenever we wanted to, without having to worry about money. I wanted a short cut to success.

I would not graduate for two more years, and our lives were fading into the status quo with too much work and not enough play. I felt that I had to do something, and I would, thanks to Microswitch! No more long hours of homework. I had a plan! It was a plan that nobody else had. It was as different as building fireworks during my teen years, but not so dangerous. My engineering friends thought it took guts, and wished me luck. I had to prove myself one more time by doing something different from the herd. Something magnificent! The job at Microswitch was only a stepping stone to my ultimate plan! I wanted to write stories. Novels. High-paying best sellers!

My first semester at the University of Colorado had ended, and the second had already begun, but without me! I had withdrawn. My "B" average was okay, but it could have been better if it had not been for the precious time I had spent working on my plan when I should have been doing homework! Engineering was interesting, and Phyllis gladly worked to pay the rent and to buy groceries. It was time to pay out-of-state tuition again, which would have flattened our pitifully small savings. My plan could make us rich. We could live like the Swanks had lived (before he ended up dead on the kitchen floor after raiding the refrigerator). I would enjoy fame and fortune seldom achieved by engineers, while our friends were still doing late night homework and trying to pass tests to get through school. I would not be a prisoner to schoolwork any more. Now I would have time to write!

Phyllis never argued against my decision to withdraw from school and go to work. She was happy if I was. It might be several months before I began to sell stories, so the job at Microswitch would be temporary. We would have two incomes while we waited for better things.

I had driven home from my interview the previous week, confident that I was the right person for Microswitch. They would train me, and I would work on new products. My name would appear as the inventor when they got my ideas patented. It sounded like fun, but the main benefit would be the freedom to write stories in the evening without the guilt of homework piling up. Microswitch only had to get one more approval from the district manager, and they had promised to call to tell me when I could start.

"Phone call for Fred. Long distance from Denver!" More pounding on the wall, louder this time.

I had located my other slipper and was struggling through the narrow walk space between our bed and the wall to reach the dressing area of our cramped bedroom. I dashed to the phone in Mrs. Stuart's apartment, trying to get my arm through the sleeve of my robe.

My hand was clammy when I picked up the receiver. I quickly brushed off dried food crumbs on the mouthpiece. "Hello!" It was difficult to keep my voice even and unemotional.

It was Microswitch. The conversation was short.

"Oh. I forgot about that!" My voice faded with a weak, "Thanks anyway," and I slowly placed the receiver back.

Phyllis was standing behind me. "It didn't work out?"

"No." I couldn't feel anything for a few moments. "They saw that I have a student deferment. They think the army will draft me if I withdraw from school." My draft board back in Illinois was inducting young men my age unless we were full time students. "They don't want to waste time training me and then have me get drafted!"

I stared through the window at puffy snowflakes floating down. Neither one of us said anything for a long time. I was thinking, "The military draft!" I felt a rage coming on. "The Government Gestapo that holds you hostage! They tell you when you can come...when you can go...when you can ____! It's like prison!" My neck got warm and I could feel the pressure rising. "I'm a lousy prisoner!" Every word of contempt in my vocabulary lined up in my mind for an explosion.

I turned to Phyllis, cleared my throat, and took a deep breath. I stopped before any words escaped. Here was the person I loved more than anyone else in the world, standing under a layer of pincurls. There was a tender look in her eyes I had seen a few times before, but had never quite understood what it meant. I knew that we could sometimes speak to each other without words. This was one of those times. Without a spoken word, she was telling me that I did not have to prove to her that I was somebody! She loved me whether I ever did anything magnificent or not.

My rage deflated. All that I vented was a sigh of relief. "I'm going to register in school again."

"School started last week," she replied.

"I'll register late."

"Okay."

We walked through the soft snow to the campus that afternoon, and I became a student again. My engineering friends were surprised, but glad I'd come back. They asked what had happened to my plan to become a writer. I was surprised to find that I could laugh and misquote Robert Burns' famous line, "The best laid plans of mice and men often 'get messed up by your draft board!'" For the first time since third grade, I did not feel compelled to prove that I was somebody!

Thank you, Lord, for the draft board! And, by the way, thanks also for that unforgettable acceptance that appeared on the face of a young woman in pincurls at just the right moment!

The Lord gives freedom to the prisoners.
(Psalm 146:7)

CHAPTER 9

A FENCEPOST IN THE MOONLIGHT

I like horses, but they do not like me. I have ridden one a few times and discovered a new kind of torture! It couldn't have been fun for the horse, either--too much slamming up and down in the saddle. They have gotten their revenge more than once by throwing me off, stepping on me, or biting me! In my opinion, horses were meant for dog food.

Some people have figured out another use for horses. They feed them, breed them, race them, and get rich. When a horse stops winning races, and gets too old to populate the stables, its owners collect one last award by selling it to the glue factory where it is "recycled." Now, whenever I lick a postage stamp, I wonder what kind of a horse it was.

I decided to stay away from horses, and it was usually easy to keep a fence between us. However, several times a week, I could be found out of breath, standing with my hands on a wooden fencepost in the middle of the moonlit Alameda County Fairgrounds race track in Pleasanton, California.

There were no horses, no cheering crowd in the stands—just mounds of silent evidence on the track which proved that the horses had been there earlier. I had the whole place to myself for a few minutes before I jogged one more half lap, climbed the fence, and walked across the street to our rented duplex. I could see the warm light of our living room from where I stood huffing and puffing in the chilly night air.

I had started a jogging program, since the only exercise I got from my engineering job was a quarter mile of walking during the day, including to and from the parking lot. When I came home at the end of the day, I only had to cross the street, climb a fence, drop onto the back stretch of the horse track, and begin my roadwork. Since this was January, it was nearly dark when I arrived. I depended on a few streetlights, and sometimes moonlight, to see where I was going.

I had just finished a lap, followed by a walk to the inner track, used for warming up the horses. The fencepost I clasped gives that past moment a present reality. Even though the post probably has rotted away, it reminds me of an event that cannot rot away. I can feel my hands on it now.....

The Bible had answered my question about what happens when you die, and it made enough sense to put my mind at ease. Now I had another question that the Bible could not answer. It was not a question for open discussion. It was too personal, because the only one who could answer it was me. It had bothered me for weeks, and although I wanted an answer, I was afraid of what the answer might be.

My question was:

AM I BEING HONEST WITH MYSELF?

A simple "yes" or "no" is what I wanted, but I could not answer my own question! I did not know myself well enough! It sounds stupid and a little paranoid to be concerned about such a thing. I knew that a "yes" answer would relieve my anxiety; but the thought of a possible "no" answer brought panic.

When we had arrived in California, my life consisted of Phyllis, my new job, our new surroundings, our 1940 Chevy, and some high hopes and dreams for the future. A few weeks later, I had asked God to move into the center of my life. I had heard for years that Jesus Christ died on a cross and rose from the dead. Now I believed it, and my life seemed to turn to a page of new happiness I had not known about until then. My hopes and dreams were being redesigned. My focus was different.

Now, in the middle of the horse track, I was asking myself out loud, "Am I being honest with myself? Can I be fooling myself? Is this 'new page in my life' an illusion that I have chosen to believe just because I want it to be true?"

I had discovered a disturbing verse in the Bible that made me wonder if I could trust myself, even if I could answer my question. It said:

The heart is deceitful above all things, and desperately wicked; who can know it? (Jeremiah 17:9)

I knew it was true, at least in my own experience. There had been times when I was able to convince myself that something was true, even though I knew it was not. There was one time when I was embarrassed to go swimming because of acne scars on my shoulders. I lied that I had walked under a welder on a ladder one day, and had gotten hit by a barrage of falling molten metal droplets. That dignified my scars! I had been dishonest with myself in the past and actually believed my story for a while!

Now I was wondering if my new happiness was so important to me that I wanted to keep fooling myself. Was I living an illusion? "Am I being honest with myself?"

I told others that I believed in Christ, that He had given me eternal life, that His Spirit lived in me, and that I would go to heaven when I died. I said that I knew this for sure, and I thought I was telling the truth. Since I had lied to myself in the past, there was room for doubt. "Am I being honest with myself?" I squeezed the fencepost and looked around to be sure I was alone. Then I looked up at the bright moon. "Yes or no?" That's when I had what seemed like a flash of revelation. The answer was suddenly clear!

"I CANNOT KNOW FOR SURE IF I AM BEING HONEST WITH MYSELF!"

That was not the answer I'd hoped for. Rather, it was an acknowledgement that it was impossible for me to determine if I was being honest with myself! I would have to find someone who could somehow measure what was inside my head and tell me. A counselor? A psychiatrist? A mind reader?

God must have known what I was thinking, for the Bible says that He knows me.

O Lord, You have searched me and known me. You know my sitting down and my rising up. You understand my thought afar off. You comprehend my path and my lying down, And are acquainted with all my ways. For there is not a word on my tongue, but behold, O Lord, You know it altogether. (Psalm 139:1-4)

If God knew me so well, the next thing I had to do was to place my concern on Him so that I would not have to carry it. The Bible invited me to do this, because it says:

...Casting all your care upon Him, for He cares for you. (I Peter 5:7)

I wondered, "How can I honestly cast my concern on Him, when I do not know if I am being honest with myself?"

There was one aspect of my life where I knew <u>I could be honest with myself</u>. Pain. If I said, "I do not want to suffer pain," I knew that would be an honest statement. The next step seemed obvious. Even though I could not touch God in the same way my hands were holding on to the fencepost, I reached out, after one last look around to be sure no one else was there. "I want to go on your eternal record, God. I do not know my motives, and I can't guarantee that I am being honest with myself when I tell you that I have trusted in Your Beloved Son, who died for my sin so that you could forgive me, and give me the free gift of eternal life. However, I know that I can be completely honest about one thing: <u>I do not want to suffer pain that would result from my being dishonest with myself</u>. Please don't let me end up believing a lie."

That was all. I squeezed the fencepost one last time, walked to the overhanging tree, scaled the barbed wire, and crossed the street to our duplex. My fear was gone, and I felt protected. God was my witness. For once in my life, I had been honest. In fact, doubly honest! Honest with myself, and with God at the same time. Even if I could not trust myself, I could trust Him.

> *... We should not trust in ourselves, but in God who raises the dead... (I Corinthians 1:9)*

CHAPTER 10

DIFFICULT DECISION

"When will you let me know what you are going to do?" Kurt leaned back in his desk chair, folded his hands behind his head, and waited for a reply. I knew the answer he wanted, but I was not ready.

"I haven't decided yet," I told him again. It had been the same conversation every day for the past week. My phone would ring. An urgent voice would ask me to come down to his office. Then the third degree!

"Can you give me a clue? If you decide to go, we have to make arrangements pretty quick!" There was a long pause while I groped for words. Seeing that it was a waste of time, he stood up abruptly, and escorted me out of his office. "By Friday I've got to know if you're going."

I started back to my office. "Do you hear that, Lord?" I sat down at my desk. "When are you going to show me what to do so I can tell Kurt?"

I picked up a pencil, and stared at a spot on the wall in front of me, trying to understand my inner turmoil. This decision would affect the rest of my life. I had to make the right one. I didn't know what to do. I had already made the mistake of discussing the pros and cons with Kurt. He was my combined coach, guardian, and manager for the first year after graduation. But he was biased! He knew how to pressure a person by telling him he would have a dismal future if he made the wrong choice.

Kurt sounded like he knew what he was talking about. He also said that his big concern was my future. There were 20 of us new grads who had finished the GE Advanced Engineering Program, Part A. The next segment, Part B, would be in Cincinnati. Kurt tried to act like we could choose to go or to stay; but unmistakably, he was pushing to get us all back to Cincinnati. I figured that he would collect a "bounty" for each one of us he persuaded to go.

"Look around! All the really important people here went through Part B in Cincinnati, then Part C in Schenectady! Their salaries are 150 percent of everybody else's! Go on with Part B, and the Red Sea will open in front of you!" I didn't know Kurt had even heard of the Red Sea! His message was obvious: pass up this opportunity, and you'll become a nobody around here!

I was pulled in opposite directions. Part A had been the best year for both Phyllis and me. Life had become full of hope and expectation! Our church was a place where we felt loved. It was a place to discover what's in the Bible and to learn how friends were applying it in their lives. I was afraid that if we had to move, our new life might fade away! I didn't feel ready to leave this nest of acceptance and care we had found. My fears were phony, however, because someone showed me

For God has not given us a spirit of fear, but of power, and of love and of a sound mind. (II Timothy 1:7)

I wanted to stay, but I also wanted to be sure that this was what God wanted, too. Several months ago, I had begun asking Him to show me in some clear way what He wanted me to do. I was really taking a risk because I knew that if I was honest in my request, I should brace myself for an answer that I might not like. I kept waiting for the answer. It had not come yet.

I heard about a man who said that whenever he wanted God to show him what to do, he got on his knees with a Bible and spent time reading and praying UNTIL HE NO LONGER HAD A CONSCIOUS WILL IN THE MATTER. When he could honestly look into the face of God and say, "I no longer have any preference this way or that," then he knew he was ready for God to show him what to do. I tried that, too. I tried describing to God how I saw things. "This is MY career that is at stake, God." Then my better sense would argue, "No! It is not! I have no career except what God gives me."

My anxiety got worse. This would be a once-in-a-lifetime opportunity! "They promise a high salary if I go. We want to buy a house someday. We can barely pay the rent now, and this is California, where the price of housing is out of control. I should go. But I can't walk away from the new life and church family You gave us. Not yet! They are closer than our own families! If I say no, I am doomed to be a second string engineer, as far as GE is concerned. A 'no' answer will limit how far I can go in the Company."

The longer I spent trying to squeeze my mind into an "I don't care anymore" state, the more frustrated I got! It went on day after day! "Dear Lord! I still care too much to be objective.

Forgive me if I make the wrong choice! I should probably tell Kurt 'yes.'"

Friday morning came. I had to tell him before the end of the day. No handwriting had appeared on the wall, or in the sky either. I couldn't find a Bible verse that said, "Stay in San Jose." Neither did I find one that said, "Go to Cincinnati." I had to decide. One more time, I got on my knees. "What do I tell him? I need to know. Please give me assurance." I waited, as if to hear a voice. Silence. "Okay, I'll tell Kurt that I will go." Silence. Then something did happen. While I was waiting, a distress came over me. It was an intense emotional pain that lasted a minute or longer. "I think that would be a mistake. I'd better tell him I plan to stay." I waited again. Amazed! The pain gave way to peace! It could not have been more clear to me. I knew that God had shown me what He wanted me to do! The sense of peace increased as the day passed.

When 4:00 PM came, I had to face Kurt. He would be upset and would press me to reconsider. "Dear God, give me guts to tell him, and to be strong." I went to his office.

"I have decided to stay here."

He leaned back in his chair and studied me with an expression of disbelief on his face. Then he flashed a quick smile. "Okay." He shifted sideways and crossed his leg. "Care to tell me what made you decide?"

After days of waiting, asking, and wondering, and finally knowing what God wanted, this was suddenly easy! "I asked God every day for the last few weeks to show me what He wanted me to do. I didn't have a clear indication until this morning, or I wouldn't have kept you wondering about me. Today I am certain that He wants me to stay, although I can't give you a logical reason."

Kurt cleared his throat. "I guess I can't argue with God!"

"I hope you aren't too disappointed," I said as I got up to leave.

"No. How could I be?" I never was sure what he meant. He reached out to shake my hand. "Good luck!"

Most of the Part A guys moved to Cincinnati for Part B. I stayed behind, fighting an increasing sorrow that even though I believed I had made the right decision, I had put a ceiling on my career hopes. I had torpedoed any significant career I might have had with the Company! They offer you an opportunity. You refuse. It goes on your record, and they never forget! But I never doubted the pain-to-peace indication God had given me in the decision.

Summer came and I was assigned to a permanent job. One day my new boss was discussing my long range interests. Then he brought up a little-known opportunity: The Stanford Honors Program.

"What is it?" I asked. It turned out that the Company would pay tuition and allow you to take daytime classes if you could get accepted for graduate work at Stanford.

A few weeks after an acceptance letter arrived, I became a "commuter student" for the next 12 years. God made it possible for me to complete work on a Ph.D. in engineering. Was my career with the Company limited? I don't think so. They appointed me one of several Engineering Fellows with the Department, which is a recognition reserved for technology leaders. Part of the responsibility that comes with this position is helping young engineers make the best choices for their career plans. It involves mentoring, coaching, counseling, encouraging, and just being available.

God has given me a status beyond the highest engineering aspirations I had. He continues to use my position by putting me in touch with hundreds of career and professional people, and thousands of university students. I can tell them from experience that if they ask God to guide them, He has a plan for them that gives fulfillment beyond any earthly promises of fame and fortune.

Kurt probably never understood my decision. Actually, his most compelling argument for going to Cincinnati was higher pay. I have concluded that no amount of money could have obtained the joy and peace that comes from asking God for guidance, following it, and watching God make the Red Sea part in front of you!

Do not overwork to be rich... (Proverbs 23:4)

CHAPTER 11

THE DAY I ALMOST QUIT

The most important engineering problem in the early 1960's was the design of safe nuclear power plant containment buildings which would not leak to the outside if a high pressure pipe accidentally ruptured. No one had figured out a way to calculate how fast steam and water would blow out of a broken pipe.

I had been assigned to work on a less important technical problem with a highly respected engineer named Art. I thought at first that this would be an opportunity to learn a lot from one of the smartest men in engineering. I did not know that I would soon face one of the worst days of my career. Art was a perfectionist. He was never happy unless everything fit perfectly into his narrow prescription of how things should be. I had never worked for a perfectionist before; but I learned the hard way that Art had this "affliction".

"Art! I think I found a way to make this work!"

I would proceed for the next 10 minutes or so describing my analysis, and giving reasons why I thought I had helped solve the problem. Art would stare at my sketches and notes, pooch out his lower lip, frown, and begin chopping. "This doesn't look like it could possibly give the right information—and what makes you think this will improve things? I think you've gone in a circle and are back where you started." It was Art's tactful way of saying I had gotten nowhere. When he was done with his red marker, my pages looked wounded and bloody! So I'd go back to my desk to try again.

Once in a while Art expounded his philosophy of life. I remember confessing the fact that I enjoyed going to a weekly noontime Bible study with other engineers. When I invited him, he scoffed. Thereafter, whenever I returned from the Bible study, he'd ask, "How was the 'seance'?"

Art had given me an interesting problem to work on for his project. I gladly spent long hours, thinking that I was helping him. Finally, I thought I had solved it. Optimistically, I showed him my results.

He studied the pages of my analysis. He kept mumbling to himself, making red X's as he looked it over. "Well, Fred," he started. His lower lip pooched out again, and then came the familiar frown. "I thought that at last I'd given you something you could do -- but I see I was wrong."

I crumbled inside. How badly I wanted to prove myself to this man -- and to myself, too! He was experienced. I could not discount his opinion. I tried to say something to hide my frustration, but no words came. I turned back to my desk, and looked down at the red X's for a long time. I wanted to walk out forever and do something else. "Dear God, what can I do now?"

Some Bible verses flickered in my head from one of the recent "seances".

> *I have come that they might have life, and that they may have it more abundantly. (John 10:10)*

> *"And we know that all things work together for good to those who love God, to those who are the called according to His purpose." (Romans 8:28)*

"This doesn't feel like abundant life," I whispered so that God could hear me, but Art couldn't. "Show me where the good is hiding in this miserable day." Then half-heartedly, I asked God, "Help me to do something worthwhile that somebody can use -- something to justify why I am even here."

I was not expecting the next thing that happened.

"Put Art's work in the drawer and take out a clean tablet." I don't hear spooky voices, but somewhere down inside, God impressed the words. The desk was clear in a minute except for a clean tablet. "Trust me. I can guide your thoughts." No audible voice. Just a strong sense that God was doing something.

The thoughts came one at a time. Two pages of analysis and a half hour later, I could not believe what I had on the desk in front of me! It was an analysis for calculating how fast steam and water discharge out of a broken pipe! It was the thing that others had been working on for months to find a way to predict! "Dear Lord, can this be happening? Even if it's a daydream, thanks!"

I tested the analysis. It matched experiments! I could feel my heart pounding. I walked out of the room, bypassing Art, to show my results to the lead engineer. He was more excited than I was! "Write it up!" he urged. "Art's work can wait."

I wrote a technical paper on the analysis. One of the engineering journals published it. That analysis became the industry standard, and was called the "Moody model"! Letters came from all over the United States and foreign countries, asking for copies.

The funny thing is that my analysis, which became well known in the industry within several months, was not a work of genius, as I would have enjoyed thinking. Anyone with an engineering math course could have done the same thing. It was as if everyone else was looking for a complicated solution and passed by the simple one.

When I have been introduced as the "Dr. Moody of the Moody Model," I make sure the audience knows where the idea came from, even though I got the credit.

Art's stuff is still in an old desk, as far as I know. He went on to solve his own problem in his own way to his own specifications. Art could not have known at the time that God was working through him to show me how He could make something good come out of the day I almost quit.

> *...I will tell of all Your marvelous works.*
> *(Psalm 9:1)*

CHAPTER 12

BUTTERFLIES AND A BAD MOUTH

I have been robbed many times—not by someone wearing a mask and brandishing a gun, but by FEAR, which can be unfounded and irrational. I'm not describing the paralyzing terror which can strike in a life-threatening situation. The fear that has robbed me most often has been the "butterfly variety," which causes me to hesitate, walk away, or try to avoid situations of discomfort, rejection, or embarrassment—like telling others how Christ has changed my life since I put my trust in Him. Most Christians I know say that they get butterflies, too. These butterflies don't go away with age or experience!

One day I remembered something my show-biz uncle said that made me thank God for butterflies. He said that his acting days would be over when he stopped getting butterflies before going before the cameras. He insisted that butterflies made him one of the best bit-part actors in Hollywood. Instead of acting a part, he lived it. Butterflies meant that while the cameras rolled, he became the character he was portraying.

I got a bad case of butterflies shortly after I started my first job. The fear of telling someone else that I had come to believe in Christ turned every variety of butterfly loose in me! I had managed to keep my faith a secret outside of church. I knew I had to tell someone, or I would have to conclude that my faith was not very real. Butterflies? Yes! Multiplying in numbers and intensity! They never have gone away! *You shall be witnesses unto me.. (Acts 1:8).* What was I waiting for?

I finally worked up enough courage to pick a target at work who would be the first outsider I ever told. It took several days. There were a few mildly religious engineers, who probably would be easy. Then there was George. He would be more of a challenge. I studied him carefully. I listened to him talk. If anyone needed to hear about Christ, George did! His foul language was worse than mine had ever been. No one could talk like that and be going to heaven! He desperately needed the Savior!

George was arrogant and polished, and he strolled around with an unlit cigar in his mouth. He also was a frequent player at our lunch time game of "liar's dice." I had joined the group because they had invited me. Sometimes I wonder if it was the right thing to do, knowing now that God hates a *lying tongue (Proverbs 6:17)*. You roll the dice under a cup, peek, and pass it to the one on your left, telling him a true or false total. If, without peeking first, he lifts the cup and exposes that you lied, you lose; or he can peek and pass it on. I never was a good liar, anyway. George could curse for minutes without repeating himself, and he also could lie better than anyone else, so he usually won the game. I planned my attack. Tomorrow!

I came to work, armed with a twenty-five cent, red paperback Gospel of John in my shirt pocket, and butterflies! I wasn't hungry, but when lunch time and another game ended, I followed George and his unlit cigar back to his desk. Then I made my move. "George!"

"Yeah! So, what the h__ can I do for you?"

"Can we talk a minute? Maybe in there?" I stepped into an empty office. George hesitated at first, then came in. "George, the Lord showed me that you are not a happy man."

The cigar almost fell out of his mouth. "What?" His voice was high-pitched, like he was choking. This had to be the power of God, I thought.

The butterflies had settled down, and I felt eloquent! "George, I'd like to give you this little book." I took it out of my pocket and turned to my favorite verse, John 3:16, which was one of the few verses I knew. "It says, 'God so loved the world that He gave His only begotten Son, that whosoever believes in Him should not perish, but have everlasting life.'" I held it out in front so he could read it too.

George was trying to say something, but it was as if he could not pick the exact words for the occasion. His forehead wrinkled from his bushy eyebrows to the top of his bald head.

"Take it and read it," I said. "It says God loves you and wants you to be happy."

A strange thing happened to me when I said that. There was an inner surge of love and compassion for this arrogant, cursing man! I suddenly cared about George! Up until then, I was acting a part. Now I was living it—just like my uncle said! "That's why He sent His Son Jesus to die for you. He rose from the dead, and will forgive you and take you to heaven someday if you trust Him."

George's eyes flitted back and forth between me and the little book, as he struggled to interrupt. Finally, he exclaimed, "Jesus Christ? I'm Jewish!"

"That's okay," I assured him. "Christ died for Jews too!"

Stammering and breathy, George began a rapid fire account of his life. He knew the chief rabbi in San Jose! Personally! He regularly attended the synagogue! He gave money to charity! He never kicked dogs, and he probably didn't have to worry much about getting to heaven if there was such a place. He finally settled down and reluctantly took the book, and even thanked me!

That was a long time ago. Since then, I have told many others how Christ gave me a new kind of life. The butterflies are always there, but I remember what my uncle said. If I ever can speak about Christ to outsiders and not have butterflies, then I will just be acting a part, not living it. "Thank you, Lord, for butterflies!"

For I am not ashamed of the gospel of Christ, for it is the power of God to salvation for everyone who believes, for the Jew first and also for the Greek (Gentile).
(Romans 1:16)

CHAPTER 13

GROUP PRAYER, A CIRCUS OR COMMUNION?

When I was growing up, prayer was something my Grandma did before the big dinner on Thanksgiving. It was also what kids did before they got into bed. The only prayer I knew went:

> "Now I lay me down to sleep.
> I pray Thee, Lord, my soul to keep.
> If I should die before I wake,
> I pray Thee, Lord, my soul to take."

Every night I got down on my knees while my mother sat on the edge of the bed, and I would speed through the words with folded hands and closed eyes. I understood the "lying down to sleep" part, but I did not know what a "soul" was. The part about "..dying before I wake," did have a morbid reality that I associated with the awful thing that happened to mice when they sprang the trap in the kitchen.

I think it was my Grandma who told me, "That little 'Lay me down to sleep,' prayer is just the warmup! You can add other things if you want to." I took her suggestion and added some thoughts of my own, depending on whatever trouble I was in at the time. For example, on at least one occasion, I added:

> "...Please help Mrs. Bean to fall down and break her arm if she ever tries to pour boiling water on my dog, like she said she would if he 'watered' her flowers again."

Mrs. Bean lived two houses down. Nobody liked her. She was always yelling at the kids in the neighborhood.

When Grandma prayed on Thanksgiving, she made up for all the times we never prayed the rest of the year. She named everything on the table, in the refrigerator, in the fruit cellar down in the basement, the roof over our heads, and long lists of other things which she had saved up for this occasion! I remember that when she finally quit, the food was cold.

Grandma also bribed me to go to church with her a few times. The minister prayed a marathon prayer when he came to something in the Sunday program called the "pastoral prayer." It made

Grandma's Thanksgiving prayer seem like a hundred yard dash! I could read a little by then, so I could see when we were getting closer to it in the bulletin. I tried to plan my morning visit to the drinking fountain or bathroom to coincide, but it was no use. I was usually trapped between the wall and Grandma, who was too big to slip past without her full cooperation. She just whispered, "Shhhh! You can wait." How did she know?

I could also tell time, so I counted the minutes on my Mickey Mouse watch to see how long the prayer would go. The minister always gave the same signal when it was over. I figured that "Ahhh---men!" was a code word, which people sitting all around were supposed to repeat, signaling who was still awake. No one told me otherwise.

There were potlucks at Grandma's church, with a kids' program following. Instead of a pastoral prayer, there was something I thought was called the "vacation". It was anything but a vacation. Years later when I could read better, I discovered it was the "invocation."

Since I must have had an analytical mind, I figured out some of the rules about prayer. Only three kinds of people could pray: Men, if they wore a suit and tie; grandmothers, if it was Thanksgiving; and kids in their pajamas at bedtime. Prayers had to contain a lot of "thee's" and "thou's", or it probably was disqualified. "Ahhh---men!" was a code word for "Over and out!"

When I started going to church with my friend Donald, my understanding of prayer broadened. Other people, including farmers in bib overalls, were allowed to pray if they were in church on Wednesday night. I had to go with Donald. It was a rigid condition laid down by his mother if we were going to build race cars and other projects. We had to sit on hard benches in a room full of people, where any of them could stand up and pray whenever, as often, and as long as they wanted to.

As the only two kids at the prayer meeting, Donald and I learned to silently convulse with laughter whenever someone was praying. Tears flowed during that prayer meeting. Some tears were for repentance, for the people who had done bad things that week, like swear when they had smashed a finger with a hammer. Other tears were for the heathen, who were lost and going to hell if people did not give more money so that someone could tell them the "Good News." (The only "good news" to me was the final "Ahhh--men!", which meant we could run outside and play on the swings.) Other tears were not quite so spiritual! That's because sometimes Donald and I were laughing so hard in whispers that we cried! Our eyes were supposed to be shut, but we usually peeked at each other sometime during the so-called sweet hour of prayer (although it never was just one hour, according to my Mickey Mouse watch.) It got to be a game of "who peeked first?" We had to bury our faces in our hands while our small bodies shook!

On with the show! Some prayed for the community, some for the church. Some complained to God about the price of bait and tackle. Several prayed in shouts, like they were mad at God, or like He was hard of hearing. Everybody in the world got prayed for! The mayor. A relative in jail. One man, every bit 100 years old, nearly spit out his false teeth, which ended his prayer abruptly. Someone behind us kept bellowing "Amen!" (there was that code word again) whenever someone else took a breath during their prayer. Someone else was snoring!

Although we would rather have been playing on the swings, the prayer meeting was fun in a profane sort of way. The fun always stopped instantly when our line of sight connected with the glaring face of Donald's mother. Her bony index finger extended at us would have turned a herd of stampeding buffalo!

A few years passed, and I moved away from Donald. The only time I prayed was in emergencies--like when my dog did not come home one January night, and when my acne got pretty bad in high school.

My praying got more serious after I met Phyllis. That was when dreams began to come alive for a future, which included both of us together forever. I knew that she had similar feelings about me. This was not puppy love! Whatever it was grew deeper, and I believed that I had to protect it, but I did not know how. I did not trust myself to keep it safe. I was afraid that our developing dreams could be lost. My mom and dad had divorced, and they had lost any dreams they might have had. I worried that dreams like ours might come only once in a lifetime. I did not want to lose them.

I thought of a solution. Bring God into the picture! I tried to do that by writing a prayer on the back of my year book photo, which I gave to Phyllis. "Dear God, Phyllis and I can't guard our love for each other alone. Please guard it with us." It was the first time I had taken something fragile and precious to me and given it to God for His caretaking! I did not understand the significance at the time; but in my lack of understanding, I sensed I had done something God wanted me to do.

We got married after our first year in college, and Phyllis worked so that I could graduate. We moved to California where I went to work at GE. We found a church where people made us feel like part of the family. They also had a Wednesday night prayer meeting! I decided to visit. Maybe it was the same as the prayer meeting at Donald's church years before, but I was different.

I joined the men who met for prayer underneath the balcony. They asked God to guide them, to give them strength for various struggles, and to meet needs. They spent the first few minutes telling what God had done, and how He had made the impossible become possible. They told of concerns they had for themselves and others. Then they prayed, one at a time, and never too long. Some with terminal illnesses actually thanked God that they would be with Him soon! A man, previously known as the town drunk, thanked God for giving his family back to him. This hour became the high point of the week for me. It was an hour that I left with anticipation of what God would do in my life.

I wanted to be like the men who prayed on Wednesday night. I wanted God to guide me, too. I wanted strength, and wisdom, as they often asked from God. I wanted God to show me how to be a good husband and dad and how to move ahead at my job. I wanted to pray like they did, but I had a problem. I could not open my mouth to pray out loud!

I had never prayed out loud before, except at bedtime with Mom. I prayed when I was alone, but never in a group. I sensed that whenever someone prayed out loud in a group, all the others were also praying with him! It was like his prayer was multiplied by the number of people in the group! Not me. I was afraid of how my prayer would sound to the group.

One Wednesday prayer meeting started out like most others, except for one thing. I was agreeing in my mind as the other men prayed. Quietly, I was telling God that what they prayed was the same thing I wanted to say, too. I was joining in their prayers for the first time in a blending of spirits, even though I had not spoken audibly. I did not feel anymore like I was just taking up space. This realization was verified by,

Man looks at the outward appearance, but the Lord
looks at the heart. (I Samuel 16:16)

It took no more effort than a deep breath, and I began to pray out loud! I was quickly disturbed by the sound of my own voice. In fact, it was the worst sounding prayer I ever heard, and I was praying it! Sweat covered my palms, and I ran out of breath. The only good part was the Amen. I was glad it was over. One of the men turned to me on his way out and said, "I enjoyed your prayer." God bless that man, whoever he was! I was certain he was lying, but it encouraged me.

My audible praying became a sincere expression to God about what I felt, in the presence of men who loved me, whether I was eloquent or not! I kept praying with these men, and I discovered a growing recognition of God working new things in my life. I wanted Him to be involved in all of my affairs. I asked him to be the caretaker of everything precious to me, just as I tried to do once on the back of a yearbook photo when I gave it to Phyllis! Only, by now I was beginning to grasp the significance.

Commit your way to the Lord, Trust also in Him,
and He shall bring it to pass. (Psalm 37:5).

CHAPTER 14

I TRIED TO HIDE

I was driving alone in the car. Whenever our only son was sick, Phyllis and I took turns going to the Sunday evening church service. This was a high time in the week for us. A little less formal, lots of singing, special music, and a Bible lesson so practical that it would have taken broken bones (or a sick child) to keep us away.

There was something hard to describe about being with several hundred people at church who had made us welcome from the first day we visited. They cared how it was going with us. They loved us, and we loved them. They were our family now. This evening, however, I felt like one-third of a person. The rest of me was back in our apartment, with Phyllis rocking a sick baby. I wished that they were both with me.

I stopped at the stop sign before turning onto the boulevard, looking to the left and right. The street was clear, except for a car half a block away, and I started to turn. The car was coming faster than I had judged (certainly two or three times the speed limit), and I accelerated while he slammed on his brakes and honked at me! We missed, but I caught a glimpse of his face that said exactly what he must have thought of me and my driving ability.

We both sped on our ways in opposite directions, but the damage was just beginning! My inside trigger released a megadose of adrenaline. All the restroom graffiti, gutter language, and sewer vocabulary I had learned in twenty-some years poured out in anger, hate, and contempt for whoever he was in the other car. I didn't like being honked at! When I finally took a breath, I was glad no one had heard me.

About a mile later, my rage had dissipated, and I became aware of how badly I felt inside. A lot of my harsh and cruel words had been punctuated with references to God. I could imagine a shocked hush in heaven as all the host peered down at me in disbelief! I had hurt God's feelings! I imagined tears in His eyes, and I was to blame! How could I have said those things? I hated myself.

I did the only thing I could think of. I apologized. I asked Him to forgive my outburst, claiming the promise,

> *If we confess our sins, He is faithful and just to forgive us our sins and to cleanse us from all unrighteousness.* (I John 1:9)

I kept apologizing the rest of the way, into the parking lot, and as I was walking into the church door. I hated myself. I still felt polluted. Peter must have felt the same way when on one occasion he cried out, "Depart from me, for I am a sinful man, O Lord! (Luke 5:8)"

Inside the church, everyone was standing up, singing a hymn. This was nice because I could sneak into the back unnoticed. I did not want to be seen, or to shake anyone's hand.

Bill was leading the songs, as usual, and the last verse had just ended as I stepped into a row with an empty place on the aisle. "Fred Moody!" That was my name booming over the P.A. system! At first, I thought it must be the voice of God, getting my attention before He struck me dead. It wasn't God! It was Bill! "Before you sit down, come up here to lead us in prayer!"

This was worse than being struck dead! How could I possibly pray? Only a few minutes ago everything from the cesspool of my earlier days was pouring out. The same voice that cursed would now bless? Hypocrite!

I don't remember my walk up to the platform, or Bill handing me a microphone. But there it was in my hand, and I bowed my head. I don't remember what I said, but it was a string of mindless words which ended with, "We pray in Jesus name. Amen." I hurried to a place in the back of the church.

I had accepted the fact that God still loved me and I was forgiven, even before the service ended. I had almost forgiven myself as well. When we were dismissed, I tried to hurry out without a word to anyone, but Carl, an IBM research scientist, stood in the way. "Fred," he started, choosing his words carefully.

I thought to myself, "He knows!"

"Fred — I want to thank you for leading us in prayer tonight! I could tell it came from your heart. You lifted us all into the very presence of God!"

Did I hear a soft laugh from heaven?

I drove home that evening, bewildered, but restored. Not by my effort, but by His promises.

*For thus says the High and Lofty One Who inhabits
eternity, whose name is Holy: I dwell in the high
and holy place, with him who has a contrite
and humble spirit, to revive the spirit of the humble,
and to revive the heart of the contrite ones.*
(Isaiah 57:15)

CHAPTER 15

ALONE AND AFRAID

It was a Saturday afternoon in the summer, and I had a cold! It was the old-fashioned kind with a drippy nose, scratchy throat, cough, and a throbbing head whenever I bent over. My emotions alternated between disgust and self pity. Rather than lose a weekend by staying in bed, I found that I felt better if I was moderately active. That explains why I was in our living room with a hammer, saw, and handkerchief, trying to put wood paneling on the wall.

Phyllis had taken the kids out, and I was alone. I was getting ready to fit a piece of paneling over one end of the fireplace when something happened that made me panic. I coughed! That wasn't new. But when I tried to inhale, I couldn't! My throat had tightened and almost closed so that the little air I could draw in made a low-pitch sound like the last, desperate breath of a dying man. I stood rigid, fighting for air, my hands still clutching the wood panel. "Run outside! No! Wave your arms!" I couldn't move! "Stand still! Breathe!" I struggled to inflate my chest with air. Then my throat finally relaxed and I could breathe again.

The whole episode must have taken less than a minute, but it left me in a cold sweat. I was glad that no one had been there to hear my performance. They wouldn't have known what to do. It would have been embarrassing if I had done that with an audience! "Nothing like that has ever happened before," I consoled myself. "It probably will never happen again."

The following weekend I still had a cold, and the same thing did happen again in the middle of the night. I was asleep and coughed. When I could not get air, I bounded out of bed and stood still in the dark, gasping! The light went on; Phyllis was wide eyed.

"What's wrong? What are you doing?" If I could have answered, I don't know what I would have said!

I was dripping with sweat by the time I could breathe again. Trying to sound composed, I told her it was just my cold, and that I was really all right; but just to have my throat checked, I wanted her to drive me to the hospital emergency room. I assured her that it was nothing serious, but secretly I thought, "If I'm going to die, it's less upsetting to do so in the hospital."

The doctor checked my throat, vital signs, and did a few other insulting things, which did not seem to have any connection with a cough. I spent the night at the hospital for observation, under a cold mist tent.

The next day a specialist looked at my vocal cords with a mirror on the end of a flashlight. He mumbled things like, "Irritation, post nasal drip, rhinitis, inflamed tissue, etc., etc.," all of which are medical jargon for his final diagnosis, "You have a cold."

"What about gasping for air? What if I can't breathe?" I wanted answers.

"Laryngospasm," he replied. "Sometimes irritated vocal cords snap together and prevent you from getting air into your lungs. But don't worry. If you can't breathe, you pass out. Then your vocal cords relax and normal breathing resumes. It's a fairly common occurrence."

How could it be fairly common? I was the first and only person I ever knew that had this affliction!

I prayed. I had tried to find comfort in the hospital Gideon New Testament, but laryngospasm is not mentioned in the Bible. The Lord healed lepers, the lame, the blind, but never someone who had a laryngospasm!

The doctor signed hospital release papers and left the room. I was alone. I don't mean that I was the only person in the room. I mean <u>alone</u>, without anyone who could understand. Something was wrong with me! And beside that, at any time I could have another episode and collapse in the midst of horrified friends! I imagined this happening in church, or at a restaurant, or at my desk, or in a department store!

Phyllis drove me home. Life during the day was normal that week, but the gasping episodes came with enough regularity that I was afraid to go to sleep. I prayed as seriously as I could every day, asking God to take away the condition. There was no change. I was afraid to sleep. More prayer. No change. I would lie awake until early morning while Phyllis slept quietly beside me. "God, why do I have to have this?"

Although my singular condition did not disappear, I made a discovery that took my fear away. The reality and depth of the discovery was validated by the fact that I could lie down and drift into a peaceful sleep, even within minutes after I had an episode.

Although I never found the word "laryngospasm" in the Bible, I discovered something called "a thorn in the flesh." The Apostle Paul wrote about some unspecified affliction that he asked God to remove:

> *Concerning this thing, I pleaded with the Lord three times that it might depart from me. And He said to me, 'My grace is sufficient for you, for My strength is made perfect in weakness." Therefore, most gladly I will rather boast in my infirmities that the power of Christ may rest upon me. (II Corinthians 12:8,9)*

I did not choose to have my condition, but because it came anyway, God used it to make me conscious of His nearness at all times. Even though each episode was momentarily upsetting, the assurance that He was near took away the fear that came with it.

> *Whenever I am afraid, I will trust in You.*
> *(Psalm 56:3)*

CHAPTER 16

A LOST HOUR?

Even though schedules were tight, Frank always had time to help me. He was a Japanese expert in stress analysis, and I went to his office many times when I needed help in solving a problem. There was always a cheery greeting. "Come in, Fred. What can I do for you today?"

Frank was on my target list for convincing him that faith in Christ would change his life. But first, I had to convince him that God existed. Whenever I brought it up, Frank laughed cheerfully, and remarked that he was beyond help. "Someday he will want to know," I thought to myself. "But I'll keep the door open until he asks me."

Months passed, and one day Frank was not his cheerful self. Cancer. Surgery followed, and I came armed with a Gideon New Testament to visit him in the hospital. Although he was flat on his back and hooked up with tubes and bottles, his voice was as cheerful as ever. The prognosis was good. "Sure, you can read some of that to me," he said when I asked.

I read some of the fourteenth chapter of John. He listened, and thanked me. "Progress!" I thought.

Frank was soon back to work, but within a few months he was limping badly. He explained his problem with engineering precision: Sciatic nerve inflammation. Then one day there was a note on the secretary's blackboard that Frank had just undergone emergency surgery for cancer recurrence. He left the hospital before I could visit him, and was resting at home.

It was a busy time for me at the end of the quarter with final exams coming up, and I had to spend every spare minute studying for them. One afternoon as I was driving home from a class at Stanford, I felt an urgency to visit Frank, even though it was out of the way. If I visited him, I would lose an hour of study time. Why not wait till after exams? I did not want to go to visit him. One lost hour of study time can mean a great difference in the final letter grade! I had to visit him, anyway. I turned onto the next street.

When I got out of the car, I saw two little Japanese kids riding their tricycles on the sidewalk. "Is your daddy home?"

"He's in bed," one of them said, pointing to a window at one end of the house.

"He's sick and we have to be quiet," said the other.

His wife answered the door. She remembered me from the earlier hospital visit. "I think he's awake. Come with me."

She took me to the bedroom and announced my visit. Frank opened his eyes and smiled without lifting his head from the pillow. His face was thin and gaunt. "I'll be back to work soon," he said in a whisper.

I did most of the talking. "Frank, I think God had me come here today for a reason." He painfully turned his head toward me. I didn't want him to think I was a circling vulture, so I asked God to give me the right words. "If I were facing the same battle you are, I know that I would find strength in Christ. But I never urged you to trust in Him. Do you think you want to?"

There was no hesitation. "Yes! How?" he whispered.

"Tell God in your own words that you believe Christ shed His blood to wash away your sins. Tell Him you want to receive the gift of eternal life."

Frank did not know where to start, probably because he had never prayed. I offered to pray, and he followed with short, breathy whispers. He thanked me and squeezed my hand when I left.

Two days later another message was written on the blackboard.
FRANK PASSED AWAY AT 3 AM THIS MORNING.
I had been worried about one lost hour of study time!

Precious in the sight of the Lord is the death of His saints.
(Psalm 116:15)

CHAPTER 17

A MASTERPIECE IN PIECES

While I was doing graduate work at Stanford, I took a heat transfer class from Professor London, a world-class expert, who was as close to a living legend as I have known. All of us who signed up for the class knew that he would expect, and we would give, more than 100 percent in order to receive the full benefit of his teaching.

The first day of this ten week class, we learned how he would grade us. There would be five problems to analyze, each one taking two weeks to complete. These would be written up as professional reports. The professor would select and grade only two of our reports, but none of us knew which two! That meant a superhuman effort on all five of them!

The first problem required a complete analysis of a heat exchanger. I had been working full-time at GE for about one year, and felt like a professional in a class mostly of students who had not yet worked in industry.

I never worked so hard on any project as I did on this one! First, I derived the governing equations. Then I solved them. Then I plotted them on graphs. I discussed how each design parameter affected the results. Finally, I did an optimization study to show how the thing could be designed for the lowest cost. When I was finished, I knew that I had created a "masterpiece". I turned in my thick report in a bright red folder. Whether the professor scored it or not, it would catch his attention. Many of the other students turned in reports that looked thin and pale compared to mine.

The following week we were already working on the next problem, and the professor returned the first project. Mine was among the group he had scored! I could hardly wait to see how much he liked it.

The first page looked like he had cut himself and bled on it! Red penned comments everywhere. The score? Twenty points out of a possible 100! I felt faint. Others around me were sighing with relief, flashing scores in the 80's and 90's.

I composed myself and studied the red comments. "Your solution to the governing equations on page 3 contains an error which makes the rest of your analysis and conclusions wrong." I had gotten the wrong solution to an elementary differential equation! All of my effort, hard work, self denial, and pain counted for nothing. One tiny error, and all was lost!

I remember calling myself a lot of names having to do with a lack of mental ability. Then I remember blaming God for letting it happen. A little arithmetic convinced me that even if I got a perfect score on the second graded report, my course grade would be barely passing. I knew that even God could not change the laws of arithmetic. He can wash away sin as though it never happened, but there was no way to wash away my score of 20!

After a few days of wanting to quit, I found myself really believing that God had a purpose in the whole matter, even though I hated the experience. My second score was in the 90's, but that only spared me from failing the course.

Two weeks before the class ended, Professor London arrived with a stack of paper. "I have decided to do something I seldom do. I am offering an optional problem about heat transfer in a rocket nozzle." He passed out a copy to everyone. "If you wish, you may solve this problem and specify which of your previous two graded problems you would like it to replace."

"Oh, me of little faith!" I mumbled. As far as I know, I was the only one who worked the optional problem.

When we say, "Glory to God in the highest," we are ascribing the highest possible "grade" we know to Him. I hope it is not irreverent to say, when it comes to turning a blunder into a blessing, God gets an A+. I was overjoyed to get a B in the class!

With God all things are possible. (Matthew 19:26)

ODDS AND ENDS

During the middle and later adult years, God continues to show me that there is no limit to what He can do when we trust Him, follow His direction, and leave the results to Him.

F. J. M.

CHAPTER 18

A PROBLEM WITH A PROMISE

"Look what I made, Dad!" My son, John, was holding a jar up to my face when I came into the house from work.

"What is it?" I asked, studying what looked like a jar of water with some white powdery stuff on the bottom.

"Mercury fulminate!" he announced proudly. He said he had made it in the high school chemistry lab, although I doubted him at first. When he described how he made it, I remembered reading about this material in a book on the chemistry of explosives. If the white crystals were genuine, he was holding something they formerly used to detonate bombs!

"Well, that's nice," I said, trying not to sound alarmed. I hung up my coat and called Lloyd, a chemist I knew at work. Yes, it sounded like the real thing. No, it's not dangerous, as long as you keep it under water. Yes, it is explosive on impact when it is dry. Yes, I could neutralize it with photographic hypo solution. I convinced John that we should keep it in a safe place. He was content.

That was not the only explosive contribution he ever brought to our family!

The phone rang one evening, and a man's voice introduced himself as Mr. Ruffle. He wanted to know if I was John's father. I was. There followed a long preamble about him and me having children together in Valley Christian School. Mr. Ruffle had a daughter, Rose, in the same class with John. Rose was adopted from somewhere in South America. Her mother was a prostitute. Her father was unknown. She had come to the Ruffle's family a few years earlier, and brought them a lot of trouble.

He went through an extensive list of faults she had, and I responded with a periodic, "Oh," or, "Mmmm!" so he knew I was still there. I was wondering how this all related to John.

"Rose has run away again," he went on. "We ground her, and she sneaks out through a window. She has friends where she goes to stay, but we don't know who they are." His voice changed from steady to angry. "Rose lies to her friends, telling them that we abuse her, and they let her stay. They are breaking the law!"

"I'm sorry to hear about this," I said, trying to sound sympathetic. "I am sure you must be upset."

He raised his voice. "Your son knows where she is, and I want you to get it out of him! If you don't, you could be an accessory to kidnapping!"

I said that I did not particularly like to be threatened, and it did not sound like kidnapping to me, unless someone had sent him a ransom note. I would talk with John, and call back later.

I learned that John knew Rose. She told John that the Ruffles abused her. They did not physically harm her, but they laid down strict rules that she was expected to keep. She ran away, and would not go back till the Ruffles quit abusing her. I knew that it was John's nature to be sympathetic. He knew where she was, and worst of all, he had promised her that he would not tell anyone!

"Maybe you should tell, for Rose's own good," I suggested. John looked offended. He saw my suggestion as breaking a promise.

"Maybe you should not have made such a promise," I said.

"Maybe not," John agreed, "But a promise is a promise."

I called Mr. Ruffle. He was not understanding. "Are you going to let your son get away with that? I want to know where she is. I'll call the cops! Make him tell you, or you are responsible!"

I tried to analyze the situation. Can you be guilty of not heeding an upset parent's desperate demands, especially when no one is in danger? I realize that in the Old Testament Law (Numbers 30:5, 12), a woman who was either still at home in her father's house, or married, might make a vow to God. Her father or husband had the authority to protect her from her own inexperience or foolishness and overrule her vow, releasing her from it. Maybe a similar principle applies to a father and son, in case the son makes a promise he shouldn't have, although it is not stated.

We had taught our sons that promises are important. God made promises that we count on. If God broke His promises, we would have no basis for hope in Him. If I made a promise and broke it, my integrity would suffer. John saw his promise to Rose as binding, although not wise. I decided. I would NOT urge John to break his promise. I would pray that God would work it out another way.

Several days passed with other telephone threats from Mr. Ruffle. When I tried to discuss the matter rationally, he would slam down the phone.

Late one evening I answered the phone, expecting to hear Mr. Ruffle's newest threats. It was a girl's voice that asked for John. Boys often called him for help in algebra homework, but girls never called so late in the evening. I acted on intuition.

"Hi! I'm John's dad. Is this Rose?" Long pause. Yes, it was. How did I know? "Rose, your dad is really worried about you. Will you call him?"

It took a while to convince her, but she eventually said that she would call him.

Rose finally went home again, and the phone threats stopped coming. Someone pointed out Mr. Ruffle at a parent-teacher meeting, so I introduced myself, hoping that things were going better. When I told him that I was John's dad, he said something like, "Oh! That's too bad!" and walked away.

I can understand Mr. Ruffle's frustration, and I am sorry that I added to it. However, I did not insist that John break his promise. Whether my reaction was right or wrong, I still don't know, and there are others who have given me their opinion, which range from north to south!

Today, John is deeply committed to be the husband and father God wants him to be. He has a high regard for promises he has made to his wife, his family, and to God. Somewhere in the background, I think he remembers a dad who agrees that promises should be made wisely, and once made, they should not be broken.

"It is better not to vow than to vow and not pay."
(Ecclesiastes 5:16)

CHAPTER 19

A BETTER DOOR

Our son Paul always has enjoyed doing things with his hands. Even in junior high, he could solder, weld, take things apart, put them back together, and make them work again. If it was something he never had seen before, he could usually figure it out. His inventive nature resulted in projects all the way from a wooden car made from bike parts, driven by a lawnmower engine, to a loudspeaker on my bedside clock so that the alarm would be loud enough to wake me up in the morning.

I was surprised one day when he announced that he would be trying out for the school flag football team. His main interest had never been in sports before, but now he was excited about the prospect. He talked about plays, practices, games, getting to bed early, and winning. While I was still wondering, I learned that his best friend Greg was trying out, and had urged Paul to do the same.

Tryout day came and went. Three teams would be picked. All those who had tried out waited eagerly overnight for the list of names to be posted.

The next day when I came home, I could tell something was wrong. I put down my things and went into the living room where Paul was sitting on the couch, staring wistfully out of the window. "Hi," I said.

"Hi."

I sat down beside him, praying one of those short, "Help me say the right thing," prayers.

"My name wasn't on the list. Greg made it."

I could tell that he was fighting back tears. "I know how you feel. But maybe there is another side that will help you feel better."

He was silent.

"I know what it's like to be left off a list. I got left off the basketball list once, and a lot of my friends made it." No response. This approach wasn't going anywhere, I thought.

Paul sighed. More silence. We were sharing the same pain. You don't need words to do that.

"I know it's tough to believe this when you feel down, but there's a verse in the Bible that can help. It says, '...all things work together for good to those who love God,... (Romans 8:28).' Sometimes He closes a door because He has something better."

Another sigh, this one deeper. " I hope so. But I don't know what it could be."

"That's part of the fun," I said with a forced enthusiasm. "I know you love God--so brace yourself and let God work out something good for you!"

"Thanks." There was a faint smile.

I squeezed his shoulder and left him alone.

The next day when I came into the house, Paul was drawing, gluing, and painting, surrounded by cardboard boxes, paper, cloth, and cuttings. Quite a mess. He was alternately whistling and humming a mixture of different tunes.

"Hi!" he said. "You know, that verse sure is true!"

"What verse?" His enthusiasm, relative to the day before, made me temporarily forget.

"About all things working out for good."

"Why? What happened?"

He stopped cutting for a minute. "They want me to be the school mascot! This is my outfit--the shield--the sword-helmet--all that!"

I fingered some pieces of his coat of mail. Each piece had been carefully cut and fitted together.

"I'll help the cheerleaders do cheers, and stuff like that. I've got to have this ready tomorrow!" He started cutting and whistling again.

I had to choke back tears of gratitude to God for keeping His word, and opening a better door--again.

My help comes from the Lord,
Who made heaven and earth.
(Psalm 121:2)

CHAPTER 20

DISTANCE

I was planning to face one of my toughest challenges—the PhD qualifying oral exams. A dozen other graduate students would undergo the grueling inquisition at the same time, and we were increasingly nervous about it. If the engineering faculty thought you had potential for becoming a teacher, they might invite you to take oral exams in five technical subjects. If you passed, you could continue work toward a PhD degree.

The procedure was historical and ceremonious. You spend one half hour behind a closed door with two professors in each exam. They put a piece of chalk into your hand, stand you in front of a dusty chalkboard, and while one of them asks questions, the other keeps score. They hammer you with questions until they find a weak spot, then they go for the throat! If you live through it, you get a phone call in a few days to tell you if you passed.

I spent an entire quarter studying and practicing for these exams. I prayed a lot, and also enlisted my family. Every evening during family devotions, we'd pray for all the things that were important to each person, including "For Dad to pass his oral exams." My young sons were not sure how an oral exam was different from a trip to the dentist, but they knew it was important to me.

Even though I had a strong assurance that God had opened this door of opportunity and would somehow guide me through, I spent hours getting ready for it. It was the worst possible time to have a family problem. It wasn't serious then, but I was afraid that if I did not do something soon, irreversible damage might be done. I had never heard this problem discussed, and I did not know what to do about it. It was a distance problem.

Dave, my oldest son was in the sixth grade, and I could feel distance growing between us. It was not the normal stage that starts before Junior High when a kid might say, "I'd rather go to so-and-so's house and not stay home to pop corn and tell stories by the fire on Friday." Dave had always enjoyed doing things with me. (When he was 31, he confessed that he had once put nails under my tires so that we both could repair a flat together!) But at this particular time, he was acknowledging me less and less. It seemed as if he were trying to forget that I existed.

I tried to analyze the problem from Dave's viewpoint. I did well in school. Dave struggled in some classes. I liked math and science. Dave liked other things. I received several academic awards and honors. Dave was recognized for other achievements. To Dave's mind, my life was one success after another, and it was more and more difficult for him to feel close to me. Distance. It was painful, and I grieved inside, but I had to block it out until after the orals.

I had three oral exams on Thursday and two on Friday. The Thursday exams went well. I had overkilled in studying. Friday was control theory and thermodynamics. I thought that these had gone well, too.

All the professors met Saturday morning to decide the fate of each candidate before telephoning us. It was cold, rainy, and depressing outside. I was at home near the phone. Dave was busy in his room and the rest of the family were out shopping. The phone rang. "Hello!"

"Fred. This is Professor Reynolds. I have some mixed news for you."

"What does that mean?"

"Well—you did well on three of the exams. But we want you to repeat the last two of them. Why don't you plan to retake them in April..."

I don't remember the rest of the conversation. This was a bad dream. I had failed? A second chance? I hadn't made it? Two more months of intense study? But it sank in quickly that this was real. I couldn't shout with joy. I couldn't even cry. I was somewhere in between. I tried to pray. "Why?" is all that came out. I had been certain that God was going to bring me through! Now I was not sure.

There was no audible voice from heaven, but two words came to my mind—"Trust Me."

Dave came into the room. "Can you drive me up to the Mini-Market?" It was raining and he didn't want to ride his bike. This was the first request he had made of me in a long time!

We put up an umbrella and hurried out to the car. Neither of us said much. "Professor Reynolds called."

Dave was staring at the windshield wipers. "Oh."

I parked in front of the store and turned off the engine. "He said I failed two exams."

Dave did not get out of the car right away. I noticed that his head was turned toward me. "Failed? You mean flunked?"

I nodded. He couldn't hold back an unbelieving smile. "You didn't make it?"

"I'll try again in April."

When Dave got out and ran inside the store, it came again—"Trust Me." Sometimes I am slow to recognize the significance of an event. But in a single instant, with the rain pelting the windshield, a burst of revelation. "Oh, God!" I whispered. "Now I see what you did!"

A few minutes later, Dave jumped back into the car with a wet bag of candy. "Want one of these?" he said, offering me a tootsie roll.

"Thanks. I need one."

The distance had vanished.

"For My thoughts are not your thoughts, Nor are your ways My ways," says the Lord. "For as the heavens are higher than the earth, So are my ways higher than your ways, And my thoughts than your thoughts." (Isaiah 55:8,9)

CHAPTER 21

SECRET WEAPONS WITH GRAY HAIR

I had three months to study for the two oral exams they wanted me to retake. It was unbelievable that I had failed the thermodynamics oral! I had done well in every thermodynamics course they offered at Stanford, and taught it for several years in the GE Advanced Engineering Program. They even regarded me as a top thermodynamicist in the company! But the examiners thought I was too slow in recognizing that they had asked me to analyze a diagram of an impossible heat machine—one that violated the second law of thermodynamics. I would be ready for anything like that on the second try.

Control theory was the other oral exam I had to retake. The subject was new to me at the time, since I had taken only one course from Professor Sharp. He had failed me on the grounds that I needed to demonstrate more depth of understanding, and he recommended that I enroll in his advanced control theory course before retaking the oral. Others had passed who were in the same situation that I was. I felt coerced into taking his second course, but there was no choice; He would be the chief examiner again. So, there I was in the front row, trying to smile and look happy while soaking up every word.

This was only the second quarter that Professor Sharp had been at Stanford. The first quarter he had been friendly and helpful. But now he was different. Intimidating. Aloof. Tough. Arrogant. The more I watched him strut back and forth in front of the class, the less I admired him. He boasted about how tough his course would be. Every time he glanced at me, I felt embarrassed and stupid. I couldn't follow his lectures, and I couldn't make sense out of my notes. But without a doubt, this new material would come up in the oral exam. Then along came Larry! God must have sent him! He was a brilliant electrical engineer who knew everything about control theory, and he tutored me through the course. I finished with a strong level of confidence.

The last weeks before the two oral exams, my boss urged me to take extra time off to study. Even though I had been studying until late every night, I gladly took this additional opportunity and submerged myself in the most intense study ever. My goal was to overkill.

Occasionally during these long hours of studying, I would look up at the wall and think, "This is my last chance. If I don't make it, it's over." I didn't hear voices, but I had a strong sense that God was assuring me of success. Nevertheless, waves of doubt were coming more frequently. Then I was introduced to three people at a Saturday night prayer meeting who proved to be my secret weapons.

Amanda, Elizabeth, and Eula were three gray-haired women who spent much of every day praying for others. People called them at all hours from around the world to enlist their prayers! Pastors, missionaries, friends and ordinary people with problems. These women waged a quiet battle on their knees that literally drove back the powers of darkness and caused miracles to happen! They were happy to place me on their list.

At my request, Professor Sharp reluctantly consented to give me a practice oral in control theory. I drove up to meet him, but he did not come. He was out protesting the Vietnam war at a rally on campus! He offered no apology when I rescheduled another appointment some days later. The practice oral didn't go well. "I don't think you are ready to take an oral in control theory yet," he said. The problem was that he wanted me to answer quickly, but I needed to think about the answers. My advisor, Professor Reynolds, had cautioned me not to be trapped into giving a fast answer I was not sure of, but rather to say something like, "I don't know the answer, but let me show you how I can work it out." Now if I could just remember to respond that way!

The day arrived. Amanda, Elizabeth, and Eula would be praying while I was undergoing the inquisition. Phyllis gave me a kiss on the cheek to reassure me of her prayers as well, and I drove to Stanford.

The control theory exam was first. I walked into the office and closed the door behind me. One professor sat behind a desk with a score sheet and pencil. Professor Sharp was smiling. Then he handed me a sheet of paper. "To get started, here is a diagram of a control system. Can you tell us the order of the system?"

Some diagrams have to be redrawn to determine their order, and they often are not obvious. "I don't know, but let me show you how I can figure it out."

"Well, I'm sure you could, but you should be able to tell by just looking. Besides, we have a number of other questions. Can't you make a guess?"

"I suppose it is a third order system, but..."

I wasn't ready for what happened next. Professor Sharp's voice boomed, "That's wrong!" He was glaring at me, and snatched the paper out of my hand. I backed away. The other professor shifted, cleared his throat, and began writing. "If you can't answer an easy question like that, I don't see how you can answer the others."

He was right! I couldn't answer. I tried, but there was no strength. My legs were rubbery, and it felt like my blood had been drained. His words did not register. "That's wrong!" kept running through my mind. I had to keep asking for clarification. This had to be a bad dream. The exam was supposed to last 30 minutes. At about ten minutes, Professor Sharp said, "I think we've heard enough." He looked down as he opened the door and gestured for me to leave.

I was dazed as I went to an empty room to wait for the thermodynamics exam. This wasn't supposed to happen like this. Where was the filling of the Holy Spirit? Where were the right words? Where was God? I felt alone.

It was difficult to concentrate on questions in the next oral exam. Professor Sharp's words kept echoing in my mind from the previous hour. "That's wrong!" If only my head would clear! "I think we've heard enough." I tried to relax, but it was like the questions were out of focus. The last five minutes of the thermodynamics exam, my mind cleared. Although I responded well to the last question, I knew that I had done worse on this second try than I had on the first try several months before.

While I was driving home, I said, "God--this was the worst anyone could have done. There is no possible way for me to have scored high enough to pass."

There was no audible answer, but there came the same inner assurance I had experienced before. "Trust me. Don't you believe that I have already determined the outcome of their decision?" I remember releasing a hollow laugh. This was behind me. Life would go on. And there was still hope that God could do this.

Saturday morning I was home alone at the desk, sometimes afraid—sometimes at peace. The phone rang and my pulse rate doubled. "Fred—this is Professor Reynolds. You passed! Congratulations!"

I savored every word, and ran it through my mind again in slow motion. "You passed!" About the only thing I could say was, "Oh! I'm glad to hear that. What next?"

He laughed. "Go have a martini!"

When I put down the phone, tears of joy began to flow down my face, and I remember sobbing for a few minutes. I don't do that very often, but I was alone, and this was the first time anything like this had happened to me. "If You can do that," I said to God, "I can trust You to do anything!"

What next? Not a martini. Instead, three phone calls to Amanda, Elizabeth, and Eula—my secret weapons with grey hair!

I will lift up my eyes to the hills—From whence comes
my help? My help comes from the Lord,
who made heaven and earth.
(Psalm 121:1, 2)

My soul, wait silently for God alone,
for my expectation is from Him. (Psalm 62:5)

CHAPTER 22

SOMETIMES YOU BACK OFF

Ed was my neighbor across the street for many years. He had a son, Cameron, who was the same age as my oldest son, Dave. Cameron and Dave were good friends through their elementary and high school years. They rode bikes, played cops and robbers, went on hikes, and were sometimes "partners in crime" together, which led to early gray hair for Ed and me. The crime part was nothing to make headlines—just smaller crimes, like starting a fire in a school dumpster.

I invited Ed to church many times. Although he was glad to have his son attend with us, his job often took him away on weekends.

Both Cameron and Dave confirmed their faith in Christ the same Sunday morning, and planned to be baptized together. Ed was happy to hear the news that his son had found religion, and promised to attend his son's baptism. He did...except that he arrived ten minutes after the ceremony.

One day Ed was taken to the hospital with a heart problem. When Cameron told me that his dad was scheduled for bypass surgery, I felt a sudden urgency to visit him. Heart bypass procedures were becoming more frequent, but were still classified as high risk operations in the 1960's. I had never talked with Ed to see if he knew why Christ died, or if he had ever trusted Christ as his Savior. He could be facing an eternity without Christ, and I at least had to explain the facts to him.

The next morning I drove to the Stanford Medical Center, armed with a Gideon New Testament. I prayed that God would give me the right words, and that Ed would receive my message.

Ed was propped up in a hospital bed with monitors attached to his chest, arms, and legs. He gladly shook my hand, and began to tell me everything the doctors were going to do. A medical team of 12 would surround him. Some would remove a vein from his leg. Others would open his chest and saw through his breastbone, exposing his heart. Dr. Norman Shumway would come in at the appropriate time and splice in the bypass segments. He talked nonstop for a long time. It was obvious that he needed to tell all this to someone, and I was glad to listen. But that was not why I had come.

"If it were me instead of you, Ed, I know that I would find encouragement in some special scripture verses." I started to read from John, Chapter 14, but Ed interrupted and started talking about the nurses. They were the greatest! They showed him how to cough after waking up to keep his lungs clear. He demonstrated.

I pushed hard to make another transition to the scripture, but Ed started talking about something else. I wondered, "When would someone be more ready for scripture than when they were facing the possibility of death?" I tried not to appear frustrated and put the testament back into my shirt pocket. "If I'm supposed to talk religion to this man," I prayed silently, "then let him bring it up."

We visited, and laughed together about our sons' antics in past days. We talked about future days when Ed would be better than new. Then a faraway look came over his face.

"You know," he said slowly, "it's sobering to think that in a few hours, someone is going to be holding my heart in his hands." He took a deep breath. "I hope I wake up from all this, but in case I don't, I wish I knew what to expect. Fred -- what happens when you die?"

I had quit pushing, and now the door had opened! I explained that because Christ died, He is able to take all those to heaven who have trusted in Him as Savior. Ed wanted to have this assurance. I invited him to pray with me and affirm his faith in Christ. He did. I sensed his sincerity. He clasped my hand, and after a long, warm handshake, I left.

Ed's surgery went well, and he made a good recovery. The following summer, he played a vigorous game of volleyball at a block party on our street. Then one sad morning, the fire department arrived at Ed's house with their resuscitator. He had died in the night. Cameron was hurt deeply, but gradually accepted the fact. Dave and I included him more often in the things we did, trying to help him through the healing process.

One day when I mentioned my hospital visit just before Ed had his heart surgery, Cameron wanted to know more. His face beamed with hope when he learned that his dad had trusted in Christ. "Now I will see him again!" Ed had never told him.

In My Father's house are many mansions; if it were not so, I would have told you. I go to prepare a place for you. (John 14:2)

CHAPTER 23

FAITH PROMISE

Phyllis and I were shocked in the early 1970's to see our credit card bill that had come in the mail! I did a little analysis. The results were horrible! What we owed, plus the monthly finance charge, minus the little we could pay would take several years to pay off. That innocent, convenient, little plastic card was the doorway to a financial black hole! No wonder I was hoping for another part-time teaching job at San Jose State University, where I had taught an engineering course the previous semester.

My hope for a teaching job fizzled. I was disappointed to learn that they could not offer a class for me to teach that semester. Even though the administration and the students liked me, state budgets had determined which classes would be offered, and which would get canceled. My class became one of the casualties.

About that time, another envelope came in the mail from our church announcing the yearly missions conference. The letter described a new way to send out more missionaries: Faith Promise. My attitude at that time was, "Don't bother me about giving money to anything, except the bank, because they 'own' me now."

The more I found out about the faith promise idea in the days that followed, the better it sounded. "Ask God to show you how much money you can trust Him to provide through you for missions this year." It did not have to be money you already had in a savings, or money you were expecting. You just prayed every day that God would provide it so that you could have the joy of giving it.

The envelope contained a card to fill out: "As God provides in response to my faith in Him, I promise to give $_____ to missions this year to help fulfill the great commission of Acts 1:8." That was no ordinary way to get people to give more money! Even though we owed a lot, that could be a way for us to see God send money through us to missions. Money we did not have. Maybe a lot of money. Money we could not keep--but it would have been worth a lot just to see it happen! We wondered how much we should fill in on the card.

A particular number stuck in my mind during the weeks before the conference. It was the same amount we owed the bank on our credit card! Why not! So we filled out the faith promise card and turned it in at the Ingathering Sunday, apprehensive, but filled with expectation. Now, where should we look for the cash?

I listened to stories of people who had made faith promises, and reported that God sometimes sent the money in unexpected ways. Kids got jobs they did not expect. Business men reported that dead investments turned in a profit for the first time. Gifts came to others. Some got huge raises. A reward for a heroic deed. A cash prize in a contest. They didn't keep any of it. It all was given to fulfill their faith promises, and they were happy about it!

I began to anticipate ways that God might send in the money. I tried to help Him by contacting another university about teaching one of their "early bird" courses for engineers who were employed full time. The chairman sounded interested. "Send a course outline and your resume, and I'll contact you."

It was several weeks before school started. This might be God's way to provide our faith promise. A week passed. I called again.

"Oh, I got your envelope, but haven't had a chance to look at it yet. I'll call you tomorrow."

Another week. I called him again.

"Oh..." Long pause and the sound of shuffling paper on a desk. "I seem to have misplaced it. Could you send me another package?"

"But school starts the week after next!"

"Well, that's true. It's too late to get approval for this semester, anyhow. Send me another, and we'll see about some other time."

Some other time? My insides churned! I wanted to tell him he was playing with fire! That he was outside the will of God because God wanted me to teach at his school to pay my faith promise, and he would have to answer to God for his dilly-dallying around! However, I bit my tongue. My thoughts about him were not very nice.

I mumbled a good-bye and hung up the phone. Then I sat still for a long time. Too late! Because of him! Incompetent! Insensitive! Someone whose word was not worth the hot air required to speak it! I hoped for his sake that he never had to come to me for a job! Why hadn't God lit a bomb under him and moved him to action? Wasn't God sovereign? Maybe God didn't care either. If God didn't send it, I couldn't very well give it. Maybe all the glowing reports about faith promise were pure luck or gross exaggeration.

I cannot forget what happened next. As I was still grinding my teeth and contemplating my gloom, the phone rang. It was the chairman's voice from San Jose State University, where I had taught the previous semester...the one where they had told me there were no part-time positions available that semester. "Can you help us? We have two classes back-to-back, and we need someone to teach both of them. We're budgeted for them, and the pay is double what it is for one course...."

Two classes? Enough for our faith promise, and our credit card bill! I could not hold back. "Dear God! Thank you."

The chairman at the other end said, "What?"

Trust in the Lord with all your heart, and lean not on your own understanding; (Proverbs 3:5)

CHAPTER 24

DOORBELLS AND DOUBTS

I dreaded it. Sometime in the 1960's, San Jose churches had a city wide campaign to send the "Message of Hope" into every neighborhood. It would mean ringing doorbells, getting doors slammed in my face, and cheerfully going on to the next house! This activity made my top ten list of "most disagreeable human experiences," which included such things as having a root canal without anesthetic.

The campaign began on Sunday afternoon in the largest downtown church. The speaker gushed with passion, insisting that people "out there" were desperate to hear about God's love and forgiveness.

"Oh, really?" I thought. Most people I had ever tried to tell about the love of God already had 'religion,' and had politely told me it was okay for me to believe the way I wanted to if I granted them the same privilege! Some had gotten angry. One man had gotten up from his desk and started toward me, roaring something about religion being the cause of all misery in the world. I had retreated to my desk and had quietly told God that I was through telling others about Jesus, and that He would have to find Himself someone else to do the dirty work. So, where were all the desperate people?

This was California! Progressive! New trends! Fun and parties! Breaking every rule of moral decency, flaunting the message, "When we want God, we'll send for Him!" A midwest lawyer once told me that he watched with interest any trend of perversion starting in California, because after a few months, it would reach the Chicago area. People desperate to hear about God? This was not the Bible belt! When you bring God into the conversation in California, it's like coming out of the closet! You, who everyone thought was a 'normal' person, are really a religious nut who is trying to make everyone else feel guilty!

I did not want to ring doorbells! No pep talk could change my feelings. Yet some people at the meeting could hardly wait to get going! They salivated over the prospect of planting both feet on the sidewalk, and charging a door with their bell-ringing finger extended like a battering ram! Getting doors slammed did not bother them, they said. These peculiar people must have been programmed to self destruct! (I think they must have been suppressing a subconscious, traumatic childhood experience!) But they insisted that they were just doing what God sent them to do.

I listened to their stories. Miracle after miracle!

"Hello! Have you ever confessed your sin to God, and asked Jesus Christ to forgive you, save you, and take you to heaven when you die? Wouldn't you like to do that now? While you still have time?"

"Why, yes! As a matter of fact, I was just going to overdose and end it all. Won't you please come in!"

One fellow told me privately of ringing a doorbell, and having the family dog attack him before he got through the first sentence! I asked him what he did, expecting that he shot the dog. "No," he answered. "I just said, 'Lord, bless this house!' and went to the next one."

I could not identify with any of their experiences. My only door-to-door experiences came in grade school when all the students tried to sell magazine subscriptions to raise money for gymnasium equipment. People did not slam doors on school kids, but they politely said things like, "No, thank you. I already have more subscriptions than I ever have time to read." Or, "Can you come back in six months when my subscription runs out?" They knew I'd never come back. The aggressive kids sold the most subscriptions and won prizes! After a week of ringing doorbells, I had sold one subscription—to my mother, who felt sorry for me. My sales approach must have been too low-key.

"You don't want to buy a magazine subscription, do you?"

"No."

Then on to the next house. I don't know what might have happened to me if someone had said, "Yes, I want to buy a subscription!" I thought it might be like going to heaven! Maybe it would have altered my DNA so that I would be eager to ring doorbells during this city wide campaign, but it never happened.

Kids still carry on this ancient tradition of ringing doorbells. When kids from the neighborhood ring the bell and try to sell something for their school, I see myself when I was trying to sell magazine subscriptions. Some of them are so young, they can't quite reach the doorbell, or make change yet. I let them stutter through their sales pitch so they feel the triumph of selling something. It is worth the inflated prices they want for candy, greeting cards, wrapping paper, and even alkaline batteries, to see their eyes get big when I say, "Yes, I'll buy one!" Too bad somebody like me didn't come to the door when I was ringing doorbells years ago!

Sometimes older kids from across town ring the doorbell--kids with tank tops and tattoos, and barbed wire earrings! They usually read the script, and want to sell candy in order to "..Keep - kids - like - us - off - the - street." If you don't buy their candy, you are giving them permission to trash your front yard!

"How much is the candy?"

"Five bucks!" They glance down the block to a parked car where the adult con artist is waiting. Extortion!

Most of the older kids show a flicker of appreciation if I say something like, "I really don't want candy. It rots my teeth. But I'd like to help YOU. Take this dollar. It's YOURS to keep YOU off the street. Don't tell your boss about it, or he will want half." They always thank me with a grin, and head down the block. I'm thinking, "Small price to pay for property insurance!" Kids have enough problems today without having doors slammed on them, too!

There are the little kids, the big kids, and the most suspicious group: the adults! I was about to become "one of them" for the city-wide campaign! It made me despise the prospect even more! When you answer the door and an adult is standing there with his finger on the bell, you know that he is not selling candy for his school. He is there either to sell something you don't want, or to cleverly rob you without your realizing it till long after he is gone. "Aerate your lawn?" "A free demonstration of a vacuum cleaner that does everything but cook dinner?" Or the guilt trip approach: "Your kids will never be at the bottom of their class if YOU love them enough to buy this family encyclopedia." "Cemetery plots before you need them to save your family a bundle of money!" "Fire alarms for every room in the house, or do you not care enough for your family to protect them?" No wonder people slam doors!

At least half of the adults that ring our doorbell come in the name of religion, and they are the most suspicious. Friendly. Charismatic. Charming. Sincere sounding. Even though they say they don't want money, I decided years ago that I must have something they want, or they wouldn't have rung my doorbell! They are on a mission to get your body, soul, or spirit, or all three! "Join us. We are a privileged few who have the truth! Don't you want to know the truth? Let us make an appointment to return and give you more information." What they really mean is that they will send out the "big guns" to brainwash you.

I did not want to bear any resemblance to these door-to-door messengers who are driven by a secret agenda. They cannot be trusted. Behind everything they say is a hidden motive. They often try to engage you in conversation about some issue of current interest. Some are intensely focused on their mission, and even if you are standing behind the screen door dripping wet and naked, they still want your view on world hunger or other plague, before they try to indoctrinate you.

Con artists? Extortionists? Deceivers? I know it's doorbell paranoia; but in my view, any adult doorbell ringer is guilty until he is proved innocent.

I don't remember who convinced me I should participate in this city-wide doorbell campaign, but I determined that someday I would get even. I was going to ring doorbells! I would stand there with reading material in my hands, and I would have to convince someone on the other side of the screen that I was not "one of them" before they slammed the door. At least I had identified why I felt the way I did. Rejection! I feared the rejection of a slammed door!

I had a widespread reputation in the energy field by this time in my career. People asked for my advice. They wanted to know what I thought about important issues. They held me in high regard. I was respected in the technology community. My name appeared in "Who's Who in Engineering." And someone would dare to slam a door in my face? I belonged before an audience, telling what I know...behind a desk, thinking great thoughts...teaching a class of young engineers, who would drink up and profoundly appreciate what I could show them...writing letters to important people. I did not belong on the street, ringing doorbells! Giving people an opportunity to reject me! Horrors!

God did not let me get away with that kind of proud thinking. I simply cared more about how people would treat me than I cared about people. If God had let me alone, I would have allowed the fear of rejection to keep me from telling others about the One who can change their lives. He knew that a doorbell ringing assignment would be an antidote for pride, in my case.

Harry and I were partners. We would take turns ringing the bell and going over a survey of ten questions, which were designed to bring a person's thoughts from whatever he was doing just then to his relationship with God. If he expressed further interest, we could tell him the good news. Otherwise, on to the next house. Harry never voiced his feelings, but I suspected he was as nervous as I was.

We joined a group prayer meeting before teams of two went out on the city streets. "Remember," said the leader. "You have water. People are thirsty. They need to hear someone tell them that God loves them."

We were shaking inside when we rang the first bell. It surprised me that most of the people were willing to answer the survey questions, even though they eyed us suspiciously. Each doorbell became less threatening. Ours was not a pressure campaign. I think that we left people puzzled because our only agenda was to help them find everything God wanted to give them; we weren't like the usual salesmen or religious suspects.

Several visits followed the "textbook" pattern. "Would you like to have the gift of eternal life from God, which He gives to anyone who believes in His Son?"

"Yes, I believe I would," came the reply from someone in the shadows behind the locked screen door.

I turned to Harry. "What comes next?"

"Maybe we should pray. They should tell God so He knows it too!"

A short prayer, a cordial "Good bye," and we were gone.

I do not know if our blundering door-to-door campaign had much impact, but I was glad we did it. It was my first opportunity to do something because it was the right thing, even though I hated it. When people are thirsty, and you have found water, the only human choice is to tell others. This is even more important when you have found "Living Water." Living in a world of deception and hidden agendas, it feels good to have a pure motive whenever you tell someone else about His love, whether you are at home, on the phone, on the street, in an office, on a plane, or even when you ring a doorbell.

God resists the proud, But gives grace to the humble.
(I Peter 5:5)

CHAPTER 25

GERMOPHOBIA

Sometimes people do funny things, which aren't really funny. Consider this example: Someone washes his hands so many times during the day that his skin is covered with blotches and sores. He doesn't just wash before meals, but whenever he has touched something that might have been contaminated because someone else touched it first. It could be a doorknob, a tool, or the newspaper. A double washing if he had to pick up an object from the floor!

I don't know when it began, but our son Paul had become a handwasher. Sometimes he washed his hands before they were dry from the last washing! As soon as Phyllis announced, "Dinner time!" our three other sons stampeded to the table, while Paul entered the bathroom. His brothers bobbed and weaved on their chairs, forks poised, ready to attack whatever was on their plates. We stalled the feeding frenzy until after we'd thanked God for the food, but we didn't pray until everyone came to the table.

"Where's Paul?" Silence. We all knew the answer. The sound of running water would stop, and Paul would emerge, holding his sore, red hands up in front of him like a surgeon approaching the operating table. He'd maneuver onto his chair without touching it, as his brothers whined about death from starvation!

The rest of us would be reaching for seconds, while Paul would be studying a dishwasher spot on his spoon. "What's this?" he'd ask. No one could give a suitable answer. Then he would arise to get another one from the cupboard without a word. When everyone else was leaving the table, Paul would be working on his third bite, painfully examining his entire place setting as if someone were trying to poison him.

"The poor kid needs counseling," Phyllis said on many occasions when we were alone. I sensed a tone of pleading in her voice. "Something's wrong."

My answer was always the same. "We don't need to pay a counselor when we can pray about it."

Money was tight, and most of the time there was nothing left over. No savings. No cushion. I thought it would be a lack of faith in God if we gave up and took Paul to see a counselor! He wasn't dangerous. He wasn't hurting anyone. His behavior was just a little funny.

I launched a prayer effort that lasted for weeks. Morning and night I fired my message heavenward, asking God to help Paul quit his extreme handwashing. Today, they call this problem an obsessive/compulsive behavior. However, we called it an irritation. I believed that if I prayed regularly, one day Paul's problem would be fixed.

The handwashing did not get better. It got worse. Paul's older brothers became more savage in teasing him about it. Paul tried to ignore them, but their remarks took a toll on him. Sometimes I saw him try to hold back tears, but he never blew up or fought back.

I prayed. Phyllis insisted that he should see a counselor. Paul washed. His brothers teased. Each one of us had our own way to fix the handwashing problem.

Prayer was supposed to move mountains, or so the Bible said. I asked God in every way I could imagine to fix Paul's problem. Nothing got better. I tried psychology in my prayers. I tried the hard sell. The soft sell. Pleading. Begging. Nothing was working. "I know that you have more important things to do, but look at his hands! He's miserable! So are we! Please heal him of this affliction!"

Phyllis stunned me one day when she announced, "I made an appointment for Paul to see a counselor." She looked like she expected me to throw a tantrum. I didn't. But I wanted to. "His name is Rudolph. They call him Rudy. He has worked with other families in the church." She seemed to be waiting for a word of encouragement from me, but she did not get it. This must have been her way of telling me that my program of prayer for Paul's problem had failed, and she had waited long enough. I kept busy at whatever I was doing, politely ignoring her, until she left the room.

Neither of us said anything for a long time, and I began to feel alone. I am sure that my silence made her feel alone, too. We needed each other's consolation, and she was ready, but I closed the door. My life was supposed to be a demonstration of faith. Instead, it was failure. I wanted to see God answer my prayers so that others would see that faith really works. But the mother's heart in Phyllis did not allow her to wait any longer for my prayers to be answered. When I saw Paul's tortured hands that night, I knew that Phyllis had done the right thing by making an appointment. Sadly, I felt like God had ignored my fervent prayers.

The nightly washing, teasing, and frustrating torments continued. "When does he go for his appointment?" I asked, trying not to sound eager. It was later that week.

Rudy turned out to be an energetic young man, who said that he had counseled many "praying families". That made me feel better, although I was thinking, "When God does not answer your prayers, find a counselor, and start the meter!"

The first counseling session was to "get acquainted." The next few sessions included testing Paul to find out "where he was," according to Rudy. Eventually, Rudy got to the whole family in separate interviews. Then he had a session with all of us together. The meter continued to run.

The counseling lasted several months, and the bill reached several hundred dollars. At the end of each session, Rudy told us that the end was in sight, and then he made the next appointment. "Extortion!" I thought, but I kept quiet. Phyllis believed that Rudy could help, and I did not want to rattle the shaky situation in our family by grumbling about how much it was costing. I decided to be a quiet hostage, and paid only a trivial amount on his bill every month. According to my calculations, it would take five years to pay off the ransom.

"Rudy called," Phyllis said one afternoon. "He wants you and me to come in."

"Probably wants me to pay more money every month!" I thought.

"He knows what's wrong with Paul. He says it's a problem the whole family can help fix."

We drove to his office, Phyllis with high expectations, and me with skepticism. Rudy appeared enthusiastic.

"Paul has a problem with anger," he began.

"Anger?" I interrupted. "He never gets angry!"

"That's part of the problem," Rudy continued. "He's got the idea that being angry is bad. When he gets angry, he holds it inside. That makes him feel dirty--infected. It comes out in a compulsive washing of his hands, and a fear of germs."

"What makes him angry?" I asked.

"Normal family things," Rudy said. "Like teasing from older brothers, or parents that don't understand. That part happens in every family. But Paul thinks it is wrong to be angry, and it is eating him up."

Phyllis and I looked blankly at each other, while Rudy looked over his notes.

"It is a cycle that has to be broken. Anger makes him feel dirty. Feeling dirty, he's afraid his family will reject him. In order to be clean, he must wash his hands. His handwashing exasperates the family, and they pick on him. He denies anger, and washes his hands. Around and around it goes!"

My skepticism was beginning to disappear. I didn't want to change my mind about this man—who cashed in on other people's problems...who people ran to for help instead of praying to God—but I had to admit that he was taking the pieces of our puzzle and fitting them together in a way that we could understand.

"We've already begun to fix it," Rudy said. "Paul told me he tried to hold his anger inside because he believed it was wrong to get angry. I am trying to help him see that being angry is OK, but staying angry is a problem. You know, '..Be angry and do not sin: do not let the sun go down on your wrath,.. (Ephesians 4:26).' I reminded him that Jesus got angry, and blasted the money changers when they set up business in the temple."

I had a disturbing thought: "Could this be God's answer to my prayers for Paul? Had God really heard me after all? Was it God's caring enough that compelled Phyllis to make the appointment? Did God give special understanding to this man, whom I had so wrongly perceived?" Let the meter run! Healing was on the way!

"I'll work another week with him on how to manage his anger," Rudy assured us. "But you need to discuss this with his brothers. You know, get them to understand and ease up a bit."

Neither one of us said much as we drove home. We were quietly savoring these moments right after the problem was diagnosed and a cure was in sight. Phyllis was vindicated in contacting Rudy for help. I gladly admitted that she was the hero in this episode.

Several weeks passed, and the excessive handwashing stopped. Paul's brothers became his greatest allies after we explained the problem to them. His hands began to look normal again.

Today, Paul handles anger better than anyone else I know. I have been nearby when I've heard him begin to laugh, and say, "Oh, no!" after he twisted off the head of a bolt when fixing his car, or done something else that would bring a burst of blasphe-my from many people. Where some things make people angry enough to smash something, Paul quickly shifts his thinking to an uncommon viewpoint where he sees such things as minor perturbations in a universe which is measured in light years.

One thing about the handwashing episode still troubles me, and I suppose it should so that I become more alert to the way God works. Why did I think that God was not answering my prayers when His answer came, packaged differently than I expected, through a counselor who was not part of my plan?

Where there is no counsel the people fall; but in the multitude of counselors there is safety. (Proverbs 11:14)

CHAPTER 26

SHATTERED

Jim could have won a prize for "the best family man without religion." He demonstrated an almost-perfect role model for husbands and fathers. "If every man were a husband and father like Jim, the world would be a better place." That was how he was regarded by others. Jim knew he was a good man, too. Whenever he was invited to church, he remarked that religion was OK for others, but he did not need it.

Jim had a deep love for his family. He worked long hours so that he could provide for their needs and a secure home. He was friendly. Trustworthy. He always greeted others with a smile and cheerful word. He knew how to make the most serious employees smile when he posed them for company photos on the front lawn, or arranged the lighting on a general manager at his desk for a portrait of distinction to hang in the reception area.

He also ran the graphics department where I took sketches to be transformed into 35 mm slides for use in technical seminars. Jim applied his "magic" and always brought back a brilliant set of slides for me to use. His slides were so eye-catching, that I could mumble almost anything while I projected them on a screen, and the presentation would be a success. Customers, people from regulatory boards, and even our company execs would compliment me for the presentation, but especially for the slides!

Jim referred to himself as an "infidel" or "heathen" when I tried to tell him how God had changed my life after I began to read the Bible. "I'm happy for you," he said. "You are a fine Christian, but it's not for me. You know my wife, Diane. She's a religious person, but that doesn't get in the way of her being the best wife and mother in the world!" Then with a tiny trace of pride in his voice, he added, "She goes to church at least four times a week!" As usual, he laughed cheerfully, and went on his way with a tripod under his arm and a camera dangling around his neck.

Diane attended our church with her children. Jim never opposed her churchgoing; in fact, he encouraged it. She taught women's Bible studies, and was always ready to help others. She was known as a caring person who visited shut-ins, prepared meals for sick or grieving families, ran errands, and helped older women clean their houses. She knew that Jim and I worked for the same department, and every time I saw her at church, she would ask me to keep praying for him. Jim had told her many nice things about me, she said. He had described me as a patient, understanding, and kind human being who appreciated the work he did. "Jim thinks you are the most outstanding Christian man he has ever known!"

Diane must have had more than a hundred people praying for Jim! Anyone who believed in the power of prayer would conclude that Jim didn't stand a chance, and it would not be long before he would come to church, run down the aisle at the evangelistic invitation, cast himself in a heap at the altar, confess his sins to God, and be saved! However, anyone else who knew Jim as I did might have concluded that the only time he would ever come to church with Diane would be in a pine box!

An important presentation was on the calendar for me. I made sketches and delivered them to Jim personally, as I had a dozen times before. "The usual magic," I requested. "Thirty-five millimeter colored slides by next Monday. I go to Washington Tuesday afternoon."

"They'll be ready," Jim assured me.

Monday came, and I was so busy on a fire drill that I did not even think about the slides Jim had promised. Tuesday morning as I collected a few backup reports for the meeting, I discovered that I did not have the slides yet! I grabbed the phone and called Jim. "I need the slides, Jim. Can I pick them up?"

"I've been meaning to call," he said, "but we've been short-handed."

That was OK, I told him. I didn't mind walking over to his building and picking them up.

"You don't understand," Jim went on. "I got the artwork done and gave it to my assistant. I don't have the slides! I told him when you needed them, and the general manager snatched him up for a travel assignment. I can't reach him, and I can't even find your job!"

I sat clutching the phone in a state of shock! The plane would leave in four hours! I tried to control my voice, but without much success. "Jim! How could you do that to me? This is one of the most important presentations they ever asked me to make! Now I've got to take crummy little hand-sketched trans-parencies! It'll look like the work of a kindergarten kid!"

"I'm really sorry, Fred. I've had so much to do. I should have given your job special attention, but I blew it!"

"You sure did! Thanks a lot! Let me know when you figure out which end is up over there! Next time I'll do my own artwork and have slides made at Photo-Drive-Up!" I banged the receiver down.

It felt like a cloud of steam came up from under my collar. A surge of acid was released into my gut. Jim suddenly had become an antagonist! Negligent! Incompetent! Unable to function under pressure! Thoughtless! Unable to keep track of his simple operation! Now I had to try to salvage whatever I could for a sloppy presentation. I hated my predicament!

I sat for a long time with my chin on my hands, taking deep breaths, trying to settle down. My heart was pounding. I closed my eyes and tried to collect myself. That was the closest I had come to an uncontrollable rage for a long time. I felt exhausted. Then I remembered Diane. "Please pray for Jim." I had seen the pain in her eyes every time she asked. "He needs the Lord." And I had just shot him down! In 30 seconds, I had showed Jim that "outstanding Christians" like myself could act like jungle sav-ages if someone pushes them! I felt shattered!

"Oh, no!" I muttered several times in a row. I had not moved, and drops of sweat were trickling down my wrist to the desk. More drops were coming from my hair, off the end of my nose, around my eyes! My shirt began to feel wet. "Are you telling me how you feel about what I said?" I asked God. "I feel terrible!" I was drenched! "What do I have to do to repair the damage?" Jim wasn't the only one I ripped up with my anger. I wounded Diane, too. After a few more minutes of contempla-tion, I knew what I had to do.

I put my clammy hand on the phone and dialed Jim's exten-sion. "Jim. This is Fred. I am sitting here at my desk covered with sweat, and I feel terrible. All because of things I said to you a few minutes ago. I am asking you to please forgive me. You know that I am a Christian, and God thinks too much of you to let me get away with treating you like that!"

There was a long silence at the other end. Then the same cheerful voice I had heard many times before. "I don't blame you. I should have kept better track. But your timing was per-fect—I was just going to pick up the phone and call you. I found your job! It was here, all finished in an envelope and I didn't notice it in my in-basket!"

The fact that he found my job, and that the presentation went well, did not make me feel much better. I went for days with a sense that I had done irreparable damage. I could only pray that God would not let me be the one who stood in the way of Jim trusting in Christ. I was afraid to speak to Diane, because I was sure that I had increased her pain. I would have to live with the scars from my moment of rage. That was OK. I deserved worse.

"Fred!" Diane was waving to me across the church foyer several weeks later. I was puzzled by the unusually bright smile on her face as she dodged people in the bustling crowd to tell me something. "I have to tell you what happened! Jim came home a few weeks ago and said something that makes me think he is close!"

"It couldn't have been because of me," I thought.

"Jim told me about losing track of your job, and how you called him to apologize. Then he said..." She stopped to compose herself. I saw tears forming in her eyes. "He said, 'If I ever become a Christian, I want to be one just like Fred Moody!'"

I did not see Jim very much after that. He left the company to start his own photographic studio in another state. One day a mutual friend told me that Jim had become a Christian!

"Thank you, Lord, for repairing the damage I did, and putting the shattered pieces back together better than I could have imagined!"

Let the words of my mouth and the meditation
of my heart be acceptable in your sight, O Lord,
my strength and my Redeemer. (Psalm 19:14)

CHAPTER 27

SIX PITFALLS

It was a sweaty meeting in the boss's office. Several of us were describing the status of a project. The pitch of the boss's voice got higher and more strained each time he spoke. His face got redder as he listened to all the things he did not want to hear--over budget, behind schedule, no additional help available, people booked solid with other work. Finally he bellowed, "I think I am going to have a stroke! My head is pounding." He put his hands over his eyes and moaned.

The meeting quickly went from a status report to a venting session for the boss. One person dared to walk out during an explosion of threats, cursing, and personal insults. The rest of us came out licking our wounds, but the boss was a casualty! Another victim of stress mis-management.

Stress! It's a word many people use to describe their everyday experience. Stress is what we feel when pressure is applied. A floor has no stress until something presses on it, like a piano. If the stress gets too high by stacking up too many pianos, the floor will collapse. There is a breaking point. However, if stronger supports are put under the floor, collapse can be avoided. I think the same ideas apply to people. Too much stress or not enough strength can break us. When that happens, we are likely to do some reckless things! I saw this happen to Rob, an engineer I met at a conference.

Rob confirmed my observation that "stress begets stress." That is, when a person is reacting to stress, you'd better keep out of his way, or he might infect you with stress as well! I think it is a fundamental law of life. Stress is contagious! Anyway, Rob let stress destroy his career, and he became an outlaw to the engineering community. I didn't get out of his way in time, and my stress response to his stress almost motivated me to cross boundaries which would have offended God.

When I first met Rob, I discovered that we had a lot of common interests. We worked on similar kinds of problems. I sensed that Rob was not happy in his job with a big company in the east.

Some time later, Rob phoned me. "I am no longer with my company," he said. "I made a great scientific discovery, and they wouldn't support it, so I left." I found out later that he was asked to leave.

"Idiots! Bigots! Stupid! Jerks!" His tender references to former associates betrayed the fact that Rob's stress level was a wee bit up from normal.

"What is the scientific discovery you made?" I asked.

"I developed a theory which explains how fast a high pressure pipe can rupture. Of course you know that everyone in the industry is working on this problem. I solved it!" It turned out that he had been peripherally associated with the problem while he was employed, and smuggled out proprietary reports when he left. "I know that your company is working on the problem, and you can buy the solution from me."

Yes, our company had worked on the problem. No, we probably would not need it. I thought our engineers had solved it already. He wouldn't listen. Rob wanted me to tell someone higher up that he would sell his analysis for $15,000, sight unseen! It would arrive by special delivery in a plain paper package.

This did not sound like the same person I had met months earlier. The more I resisted, the more demanding Rob grew. The "stress begets stress" principle began to work on me. I could feel myself getting upset. I was being used. I was being coerced to do something I did not want to do. He had no right to ask such a thing! He was out of bounds! I reacted! And I later found out that my reactions are named on a list of violations that God hates! Here is the list:

> These six things the Lord hates. Yes, seven are an
> abomination to Him:
> A proud look,
> A lying tongue,
> Hands that shed innocent blood,
> A heart that devises wicked plans,
> Feet that are swift in running to evil,
> A false witness who speaks lies,
> And one who sows discord among brethren."
> (Proverbs 6:16-19)

I'm glad I found this list, because I have lived dangerously close to each violation. The process usually involves pitfalls, which I can fall into if I allow myself to be lured. If I tumble into one, it is by choice, and I don't want that to happen. Stress plays a major role.

Here was a voice on the telephone, pushing me close to the edge of these pitfalls, where I could have done damage! I guess I can't give Rob credit for putting me in jeopardy. After all, I was holding the receiver to my ear by choice. This is what happened:

PITFALL #1   *A proud look:*

I could feel my ears get warm as I thought, "Who does he think he is, asking me do do his dirty work! Doesn't he know who he is talking to? I have a good reputation in the industry, turning out important analyses, and he is a little-known, disgruntled engineer who wants me to take my precious time and waste it on his bootlegged analysis! He's nuts!"

I'm glad I didn't say what was in my mind! Just thinking it was bad enough, because the first thing on the list that God hates is "..a proud look." (Proverbs 6:17a) That described my state of mind as the stress was rising.

I tried to derail Rob by suggesting, "I don't think anyone will want to buy an analysis they can't examine first. People don't usually buy things that way, unless there is a money-back guarantee!"

His tone grew arrogant, explaining that this analysis was his "ace in the hole", and that many big companies would want to buy it. Furthermore, I should be grateful that he was giving us the first opportunity!

"I'd be a fool if I let you examine it first," he snapped. "I am not going to take a chance on some big company stealing my analysis!" He was convinced that it was his analysis, even though he was the one who stole it! "I know how big companies operate! They steal it first, then send it back with a 'No, thank you' note, and get it without paying for it! Tell them my offer, and I'll call you in a couple of days." He hung up.

PITFALL #2   *A lying tongue:*

Rob was 3000 miles away. I could ignore his request, and tell him I tried to sell it, without actually wasting anyone's time on it. It would just be a "white lie", and his arrogance did not deserve more than that from me. I was surprised that I even had that thought! The second thing on the list that God hates is, "...a lying tongue." (Proverbs 6:17-b)

I begrudgingly discussed Rob's proposal with several managers in the days that followed, chiefly so that I could tell him honestly that I carried out his request. They looked puzzled at me. "Do you really think that we need that kind of help?" Of course I didn't, and maybe my own people were associating me with the bizarre proposition. "We solved the problem months ago! You honestly think we should pay in advance for a package in a plain wrapper? Is he in the dirty pictures business?"

PITFALL #3   *Hands that shed innocent blood:*
Something I considered a mild reaction turned out to be equal to murder in God's view! I felt a panic to do something fast. My coworkers might have been thinking that I was promoting Rob's idea, and that is the last thing I wanted them to think. I can understand Peter's reaction in the Bible when he was afraid to be identified as a disciple of Christ. He began to curse and swear, saying he did not know Him! (Mark 14:71) I wanted to do the same thing, and tell them, "The guy is a fool, who won't take no for an answer until I insult your intelligence with his asinine proposal." This would be my disclaimer to show I had no ties with him.

I bit my tongue, probably because somewhere in my head I remembered that calling someone a fool had a serious connection with murder! Regarding another person as a worthless, empty-headed creature apparently raises eyebrows in heaven! I looked it up later and found that when you call someone a fool, you are telling God that a person He created, values highly, and died for, is junk! God sees it as equivalent to murder!

> *You have heard that it was said to those of old, 'You shall not murder', and whoever murders will be in danger of the judgment. But I say to you that whoever is angry with his brother without a cause shall be in danger of the judgment. And whoever says to his brother, 'Raca!' (empty head) shall be in danger of the council. But whoever says, 'You fool!' shall be in danger of hell fire. (Matthew 5:21, 22)*

The third thing on the list that God hates is, "...hands that shed innocent blood." (Proverbs 6:17c)

Rob was not innocent, even by ethical standards. But his "crime" did not give me license to consider him a fool.

PITFALL #4   *A heart that devises wicked plans:*

I seldom think of getting revenge, but this situation was tormenting me. I developed a paranoia about answering the phone, thinking that each incoming call would be Rob. I was not afraid of him, but I was afraid of how I might respond. The phone rang a few few days later. It was him.

I tried to explain what happened in a gentle way, assuring him that it was a business decision not to purchase his analysis. We were grateful for being considered first, and we did not doubt that he had found a bona fide solution. But we also had a solution, and did not need a second one. Furthermore, we would be the first to wish him "good luck" as he made other calls on all the other companies out there who were (to use his words) "desperate for the solution."

I should have ended the conversation right then, but I was too slow. The rage had begun! The telephone cord must have been close to melting!

"Your company could not have solved it! It's a bluff on the part of your management! The problem is too complicated. I have the only solution!" The noise coming from the receiver was so loud that I could lay it on the desk and still hear well!

I have seen remarkable results from one of the proverbs, which says,

A soft answer turns away wrath,
but a harsh word stirs up anger. (Proverbs 15:1)

I tried the soft word approach. "I'm sure you have the solution, Rob, but our guys here aren't exactly second-rate. They found a solution that is all they need for power plant accident analysis."

"I don't think you tried hard enough to get them interested!" he accused.

"Look, Rob, I don't even work in that group that says they solved the problem. But I know that we are not trying to sell their solution. They won't be competing with you. Why don't you just sell it to all the other companies out there that you mentioned? I'm sure they will be interested."

He began to curse and swear and call me names. Someone from an adjacent office was standing in the doorway, with a puzzled look on his face. He made signs and mouthed the words, "Why are you holding the phone so far away from your ear?" I held the receiver out to him. He shook his head. "I'm in my office if you need me!"

I could hear Rob's voice, but I was not listening to his words. Instead, I was thinking, "How can I hurt this guy?" I wanted to even the score! I could not let him get away with all that gutter blasphemy directed against me! I had to do him harm! I had to get even!

I came dangerously close to the the fourth thing that God hates: "..A heart that devises wicked plans." (Proverbs 6:18a)

PITFALL #5 *Feet that are swift in running to evil:*

"Rob!" I interrupted. (He had raved on for three minutes!) "I don't think you will sell your analysis without first showing what it can do!"

"Nobody gets to see it! They'd love to see it, wouldn't they, so they could steal it! Then I would be out! They'd like that, wouldn't they!"

This guy has crossed the line of rationality, I thought. I owed it to the industry (and the rest of mankind) to let the world know what kind of person he had become! I would start with his former employer, then to people in key positions where he might try to sell his stolen analysis. I would be serving others by sounding the alarm!

By this time, my heart was racing, and I could anticipate the satisfaction of spreading the word about him as soon as I got him off the phone! That unconverted part of me called the "flesh" loves to tell others bad news about someone else who is not there to defend himself. It is sometimes called gossip. I knew that I could not do that and still look at my face in the mirror! Besides, any rational person who listened to Rob would realize that he was out of bounds. They did not need me to tell them. If I did, I would be contributing to his hurt. That would be evil, purposely hurting someone else who obviously needed professional help! The fifth thing God hates is, "...feet that are swift in running to evil." (Proverbs 6:18b)

PITFALL #6 *A false witness who speaks lies:*

He continued a lively tirade, punctuated with expletives, that sounded at times like self-pity, self-defense, and prophecy that "They would get theirs!..." Then he slammed down the phone, and that was the last time I heard his voice.

I had to sit still for a while. It bothers me whenever someone is angry, upset, disappointed or impatient with me. Something inside wants to fight back and run away at the same time. In so-called professional circles, the fighting is usually not with fists and loose office equipment. It often involves making statements which range from an outright lie, or leaving out facts, or otherwise slanting the truth, so that the reputation of someone is damaged. It happens all the time in political campaigns. It is called slander. I have done it! Tone of voice. Body language. A little acting. I can draw sympathy, vengeance, pity, anger, or whatever I want if I choose my words and actions carefully.

Rob's reputation was self-destructing, and just then, I wanted to help him finish the job! I could have broadcast his reaction to me in such a way that others would shun him. I could have told the facts, but by withholding other information...by not stating that this was not the Rob I used to know, and that something must have happened to upset him terribly, I would be a false witness! The sixth thing God hates is, "..A false witness who speaks lies." (Proverbs 6:19a)

My emotions had settled by lunch time. I could see more clearly. God had enabled me to avoid tumbling into the pitfalls where it would have been so easy to commit the violations God hates:

> Pride. (Who does he think he is?)
> Lying. (It would just be a "white lie.")
> Bloodshed. (The guy is a fool!)
> Wicked plans. (How can I hurt this guy?)
> Running to evil. (I had to tell the "world" about him.)
> False witness. (Withholding information.)

There is a seventh violation God hates in the list of Proverbs 6:16-19, noted as "..one who sows discord among brethren." This may be the most serious of all violations, for it involves hurting those who belong to God through faith in Jesus Christ. They are His own blood-bought property, and He cares what happens to his own!

It is upsetting to me that the "stress begets stress" principle was illustrated so dramatically when I allowed one suffering engineer to move me close to six of the seven violations God hates. However, I suppose that if I am upset, I am more careful to avoid the pitfalls.

The last I heard about Rob was that he was still unemployed, living in the Midwest with a brother. A casualty of stress.

I must have been a casualty of stress, too, because I never made an effort to call him back to tell him I cared. Actually, I did not care. Not until my wounds healed that he had inflicted. I could have told him that Christ cared about him. Maybe he would have hung up on me again, but that's the risk you take any time you reach out to someone.

For You have delivered my soul from death. Have you not delivered my feet from falling, That I may walk before God in the light of the living? (Psalm 56:13)

CHAPTER 28

GOLDEN OPPORTUNITY

One day I was opening the mail. "Congratulations! You have been selected as this year's recipient of the Westinghouse Gold Medal for pioneering work in nuclear reactor safety."

I read it a second time. Then a third. I checked to be sure the letter was addressed to me. "The award will be presented to you at the Joint Power Generation Conference (JPGC) in Phoenix."

This had to be a rare occurrence—a GE engineer being awarded a Westinghouse medal! GE and Westinghouse compete in many markets. It's war! Light bulbs, motors, generators, appliances, and nuclear reactors! My boss thought it was great! "Sure, you can go! We'll pay your way."

I would have liked to relax, show up for the award, smile for the flash bulb, and take the next plane home to show off the medal. But from somewhere deep inside my memory came the verse:

To whom much is given, from him much will be required.
(Luke 12:48)

I read the list of other previous recipients: Presidents of companies; successful men who started their own institutions; each person named had achieved fame and fortune, and some were legends in their own time, like Admiral Hyman Rickover! God had to have a sense of humor, making my name appear on this list! "Fred Moody. Engineer, who analyzed two-phase steam/water critical flow. A nice guy who drives an old car." I began to worry about what strings God had attached to this happening.

I had attended award ceremonies before, and observed two general responses from those receiving awards: the *minuteman* response; and the *academy award* response. The minuteman response describes those who rumble up to the podium, shake hands, receive the award, pause and look dignified for the camera, mumble a thank you, and rumble back to their chairs while the applause fades. It takes about a minute. The academy award response is like that of the minuteman, except that it includes an acceptance speech which gives credit to all family members, living or dead; to the boss; to the company; to the Society; and in extreme cases to God, angels, and the devil so that no one would feel left out.

As I was trying to imagine what I could say, the phone rang. It was from Society headquarters in New York.

"This is Herb T., in charge of Society meetings and special events."

I assured him that I planned to come to Phoenix.

"You know," he continued, "there is no special speaker at the luncheon where your award will be made. Considering the magnitude of this award, it would be appropriate for you to give a 15 minute talk." This was the string attached! He did not specify a subject, so I spent the next weeks praying for something appropriate to occupy 15 minutes.

I arrived in Phoenix and checked into the hotel one day before the awards luncheon. The phone woke me up the next day. It was a close friend in San Jose, calling to tell me he was praying for me! That phone call charged me with confidence that God would give me just the right words for the audience. I felt like Daniel. "Bring in the lions!"

My bravery deflated when I saw the room which was decorated for the luncheon. It was the main ballroom with over 600 place settings! This was not like my typical class of 20 or 30 students that I was used to facing.

People began to gather. An ultra-polished gentleman in a dark, tailor-made business suit introduced himself as the president of the Society. He took a few notes about my background. "We have several presentations today. It will be a brief, fast-moving program," he stated, fully in charge.

I asked, "Did you know that Herb T. called several weeks ago and told me to prepare a 15 minute talk for this event?"

Then came a surprise I was not expecting. The president smiled, as if he knew something I didn't. "I'm sure that your peers at this luncheon will appreciate it if you forego any speech." He walked away.

I did not know whether to feel relief or anger at the agonizing I had done trying to put a speech together, which would not be given now. Somebody got the wrong message. Did I misinterpret this once-in-a-lifetime opportunity? Herb T., whoever he was, said to give a talk. I believed that God wanted me to express more than the usual handshake. But the Society president said to keep quiet. Had I come this far only to be a..."minuteman?" I knew that God would understand. But this was not the only surprise to come.

When the lunch was over, the president made welcoming remarks from an elevated stage. While he was speaking, my thoughts stumbled over a verse of scripture I had read before coming down from my room to the meeting:

> *Fear not, for I am with you; Be not dismayed, for I am your God. I will strengthen you, yes, I will help you, I will uphold you with My righteous right hand.*
> *(Isaiah 41:10)*

I began to shiver. This was Phoenix! In the summer! I hoped that no one saw.

Next, the president said a few words about the Westinghouse award, and announced my name as this year's recipient. He motioned for me to come up to the platform. "Minuteman!" I thought. Nothing to shiver about. "..I am with you..."

The president handed me one flat box and held up another. "The one you are holding is the real thing. You put that in the safe. This other one is a bronze replica to display."

I automatically took the gold medal out of the box and held it up for the audience to see. It was a three inch medallion. After taking a long, careful look, I said what I had not planned to say. "The Bible says that the streets in heaven are paved with this stuff!" The words kept coming. I knew that I had to shut up quickly, but there was no logical place to stop talking and sit down! The audience was warm and responsive. That inspired me to keep going, even though I was faintly aware of the cold, dark figure standing behind me with his arms folded.

I extolled the character of George Westinghouse, and told how God had sent people with similar virtues into my life to mold my values and career. I told about the GE Bible study. A career with purpose. How God can take a life and multiply it like the loaves and fishes on the shores of Galilee. "And one day, I hope to see you all again where we can walk together on this material."

The audience applauded. When I turned, I looked into the glaring face of the president. He was not applauding. I quickly slipped back to the table while he proceeded with the other awards. And then I began to shiver again. I imagined that the president would swoop down after the meeting was over and tell me that this was not a religious ceremony, and that I spoiled the whole thing by my remarks.

When the meeting was dismissed, I started for the door, but the direct route was quickly blocked with people pushing back their chairs and standing up. I braced myself, expecting the worst. Someone grabbed my hand and shook it. "Congratulations! Thanks for your testimony!" An arm reached around my shoulder. "It took guts! God will bless you for it!" "Praise the Lord for people like you in our profession!" The president never got to me!

I wondered if a smoking letter would come from the Society, but it did not. Instead, several letters came which confirmed that God had been in control from the beginning. Here are a couple of excerpts:

> "In rushing to catch a plane, it was my loss in not getting to meet you. Congratulations on the award. Your talk was the high-light of the JPGC." E.L.B.

"..There can't be many tougher audiences for this message and I commend you for not only drafting a sound and compelling statement concerning the importance of putting God out in front, but also for an eloquent and sensitive delivery that must have touched many empty and needy hearts. Your remarks hit me at a time when I needed just that kind of bold Christian encouragement. Thank you." R.W.B.

But His word was in my heart like a burning fire
shut up in my bones; I was weary of holding it back,
and I could not. (Jeremiah 20:9)

CHAPTER 29

TOUGH MAN

My specialty at work had become unsteady flows, often involving hot water discharge from ruptured pipes. My job was to calculate the reaction forces so that the structural engineers could make the containment design strong enough. The Nuclear Regulatory Commission (NRC) watchdogged all containment calculations by hiring outside experts to check results. If there was notable disagreement, meetings were called in Washington for the experts to fight over who was right, with the NRC refereeing.

I did not want to make mistakes in my calculations. That is why I checked, double-checked, consulted, and prayed a lot about the results I transmitted for various projects. One calculation I did was a first-of-a-kind force prediction to ensure that a 40 foot tall nuclear boiler would not be pushed over if a pipe should break. In this case, the utility who owned the boiler had already used my results to pour concrete before the NRC had time to examine my results.

The phone rang. "Fred, the NRC has done a computer check on your calculation." The voice on the other end was slightly frantic. "They calculated higher forces than you did, and they want immediate resolution. Otherwise they will not allow the plant to start up!"

I groaned. Whenever calculations are done by computer, the pages of printed output give it a look of authenticity. My calculations often were done more simply, sometimes with just pencil and paper, but with built-in conservatism.

"You have to go to Washington to resolve this," the voice continued with little composure. "Fly Tuesday for a P. M. meeting with the utility executive vice president, Mr. Dunker. Wednesday, meet with the NRC."

I was relatively calm about my calculated results. I might have to convince people that the NRC computer program they used was not right for this calculation. But—me against the computer? Was that the real purpose of this mission? "God knows all about this," I reasoned. "He must have another purpose."

I had met many engineers and officers in the energy indus-try whose identity was their job. Take that away, and there would be nothing left but a skeleton! They needed God in their lives, and sometimes they listened politely when I told about how He had changed my life. Probably the Lord was sending me to tell someone in particular, whom I might never meet under ordinary circumstances. "Maybe a co-worker, a seat partner on the plane, a taxi driver,..." I felt a surge of nerves. "Maybe a util-ity executive vice president?"

I arrived at night with the project and licensing managers, and we went to the hotel. Mr. Dunker had reserved a small din-ing room for our P.M. meeting, and he had also ordered dinner and a portable bar.

We entered the dimly lit room where a dozen or so utility rep-resentatives were standing around the bar, loosening up. One man in a dark suit was standing alone with a drink in his hand. The others seemed to purposely keep some distance from him. He started toward me, extended his hand, and greeted me. He was not smiling. "Are you Fred Moody?"

I admitted that I was. I was shaking hands with Mr. Dunker for the first time.

It was the way he asked his next question that made me realize I had underestimated the importance of this mission, at least to the man who was now searching my face with penetrat-ing eyes. "Are we OK?"

If my calculations were wrong, it would cost a lot of money to fix, and for every day a utility is delayed, it can cost up to a million dollars. It would be like personal money out of his pock-et if I were wrong.

I gave the only appropriate answer. "Yes, I think so."

His face immediately broke into a relieved smile, and he invited me to sit across the table from him during the dinner. He had difficulty maneuvering his tall frame into a chair, not because it was wedged between the table and a wall, but because he had already made numerous trips to the bar while waiting for us to arrive. The representatives sitting on his right and left gave him plenty of room.

I had heard about this man. A highly regarded, much feared, intimidating, tough executive. An engineer by training. Brilliant. You didn't try to fool him. It was known that he could out-drink most others at night and be sharp and alert by morning, while they were still nursing hangovers. Besides, he had power. If he told a corporation to jump through a hoop, they jumped. At this particular time, he was also a man with a breath-alcohol-content so high that it could take paint off a wall, and we were face to face!

I was fumbling with the salad, answering questions like where I went to school, my years of experience, and why I thought my calculations were right. Between questions, I was pondering. "This man has confidence in me. What will he think of me if I try to steer the conversation toward the love of God?" I was more nervous about what he might think of me than I was about fighting in the technical arena the next day.

The waiter kept his glass full. "I'm afraid of him!" I finally admitted to myself. "What if he complained that our general manager had sent a religious nut to save his soul for Jesus? My reputation could sink out of sight! The Lord had to be sending me to someone less intimidating. There were Christian executives He could send to reach their own kind, including Mr. Dunker!

I was not ready for his next question. "Bernie says that I can trust you because you read your Bible and pray. Is that so?"

I almost choked! Bernie was the project manager who blabbed a lot! I reasoned that an affirmative answer would not seriously damage our company's image. "Yes, I do." But somehow I could not find words to follow up.

Mr. Dunker was attacking a New York steak that seemed to keep getting away from him. Finally he speared a piece on the end of his fork, and carefully examined it. "Why?" He asked, continuing to study it, turning it this way and that. "Why do you read your Bible?"

That question was an open door big enough to drive a bus through. I felt a rush of energy, took a deep breath, and began to explain why I read the Bible. "I have found a new kind of life in the Bible," I said. "That Book changed my life, and gives me hope. In fact, it gives purpose to everything that happens to me." His fork had stopped moving. "When you discover One who loves you enough to die for you, it changes you." I waited. It was too late to backtrack. I was a religious nut, now. But he had asked me about it, and it would have been disrespectful not to answer! Both barrels! "In case you never heard, Mr. Dunker, Jesus Christ loves you and died for your sin so that you can have the gift of eternal life."

He was looking directly at me. Actually, he was looking *through* me! No words. Not a flinch. His eyes were glassy with yellow, green, and pink reflections. Maybe he was asleep with his eyes open, although I could not be certain.

Another voice rose above the muttering all around us. "Tomorrow--eight o'clock at the NRC."

The next day I explained my analysis to the NRC and why I thought the computer program they had used to check it did not give the correct result. My discussion was well-received without much resistance. Mr. Dunker sat with the observers. Our departure was hurried, but he shook my hand vigorously, and communicated his appreciation and approval to our team. Then we were homeward bound.

I wondered about God's purpose for this mission as we flew home. Was it to settle a technical issue? Was it to save a lot of unnecessary expenses which would have resulted if I could not have shown that my calculations were correct? Or did He send me just to tell one tough, lonely, heavy drinking utility executive that God loved him?

Always be ready to give a defense to everyone
who asks you a reason for the hope that is in you,
with meekness and fear. (I Peter 3:15)

CHAPTER 30

PROJECT MOM

The doorbell rang one night when I was in my third year of high school. I was upstairs working on a project in my room and Mom answered the door. I could hear a deep, masculine voice. Whatever I was doing had me so engrossed that it startled me when I heard Mom's voice at the foot of the stairs, calling for me to please come down.

I was greeted by a big man in an overcoat, who turned out to be a police detective. "Son, please let me see your hands." I held them out without hesitation. He took a quick look, and said, "I'm sorry to bother you both. At least five times a week Mrs. Bean calls us with some complaint! She did not outright accuse your son, but she thought he might somehow be involved."

"Someone threw red paint on Mrs Bean's house tonight," Mom informed me. "But I knew that you would never do anything like that!"

I tried to act mildly shocked that anyone would do such a thing, then politely excused myself to "..finish my homework." Mom was beaming and showed our guest to the door as he kept on apologizing. I suddenly realized that the detective was looking for traces of red paint on my hands, which I had removed earlier with turpentine! I never discussed it further, because I did not want to shatter Mom's image of me!

Since my dad had divorced Mom, I had been elevated in her eyes as the only man in the world who was worth any significant sacrifice she could make. Sacrifice she did! She gave my sister, Joyce, and me all the things the other kids with *two* parents had! Ballet lessons for Joyce, bicycles, money for movies, tumbling lessons, art lessons, summer camp, and a ton of presents at Christmas. She bought a used car for my high school graduation so that I could have something to drive to college! She was always in debt.

The only reason I went to college is because Mom wanted me to go. She wanted me to have "..all the opportunities she missed by not going." She had saved $350 over a nine-year period to help pay for the first semester. I was hooked on the education thing when the second semester came. Mom had to cash in some bonds, which were the rest of her savings. Then she started another account for Joyce to start college someday!

Mom believed in me. Whatever God has permitted me to become today, I realize that he used her to get me started. She enrolled me in Sunday School, to be sure I would be "well-rounded," although she seldom came to church. Her religion was a popular heresy, which would be easily recognized by many. I will refer to it only as "The Cult". The widespread mail-order plague of The Cult kept her supplied with booklets on every subject of human interest. I read a lot of their material, which was abundantly available on lamp tables and bookcases around the house. I did not realize that The Cult used only parts of the Bible and considered some of its fundamental teachings irrelevant! Neither did I realize that by standards of the Bible, The Cult was nothing less than sugar-coated poison!

Four years after Phyllis and I were married, we were living in San Jose where I worked at GE, and our first son was born. We also were on a steep learning curve as we studied the Bible in a young adult Sunday School class. It took a few months for me to make the connection, but it began to trouble me that Mom, who had invested so much in me, might be shackled in a false religion! I did not have any material from The Cult to study so that I could determine if they really taught the Bible, so I decided to write them directly, asking them where they stood on certain issues. My letter went something like this:

> "I read a lot of your material when I was growing up. I had bad acne in high school one year and wrote to you for help. You wrote back and said your prayer groups would pray for me. You even sent me a pamphlet which encouraged me through that difficult period. But you never say anything about the death of Christ on the cross or His resurrection. You never mention that faith in Christ is necessary for salvation. You never mention hell, or judgment, or that receiving Christ as Savior is essential for receiving forgiveness. Please tell me where you stand on these issues."

They sent a pamphlet to me. It said that God was too loving to make a hell, and Jesus was either in pain or delirious when He said certain things that we should ignore. Sin, sickness, and old age, and death are inventions of man, and not realities of God.

That did it! No doubt remained. If Mom believed the teachings of The Cult, she was missing the main thing...salvation by faith in Christ. She was lost! All the good she had given to my life could not erase the fact that she was lost!

I went through several days before I could accept the possibility that my mother, who wanted to give me the best life possible, could be missing the life which God wanted to give her! The Bible left no compromise, however.

> *For I delivered to you first of all that which I also received: that Christ died for our sins according to the Scriptures, and that He was buried, and that He rose again the third day according to the Scriptures.*
> *(I Corinthians 15:3,4)*

I had to tell her. I could not rest until I did.

Her response to my five-page, typewritten letter was a newsy letter describing what my sister was doing, how the family dog and Grandma were growing older, conditions in the automobile agency where she worked, and news about the neighbors, including Mrs. Bean, who never had a good word for anyone. And, by the way, she was glad we had found a church, and she was always happy to get letters from us!

I wrote another letter, asking her to accept Christ as her personal Savior. She sent us another neighborhood news letter. I kept writing. She kept answering, but without reference to my pleading with her to abandon The Cult and read the Bible. "Maybe she is so busy she only has time to read the greeting!" I thought. We were planning a trip back to Aurora in a few weeks. I would discuss it with her then.

We were sitting in her living room when I brought up the subject of religion. Mom said, "Your sister and I have had mixed emotions about your coming to visit. Did something happen to you?"

"I found an entire missing link in my life," I told her. "Something The Cult never writes about. Mom, I want you to be saved."

I must have said the wrong thing. Her eyes grew wide and she shrieked, "Saved from what? What is there to be saved from? Do you think I don't know that God is love? As long as He is love, what is there to be saved from?"

I tried to stay calm. "From sin. From hell."

"I can't believe that my own son has become a religious fanatic! You're talking like Donald's mother, 'Mrs. Hellfire and

Brimstone', used to talk! Everybody is some kind of sinner. She never could find anything good in any person!"

"Mom," I pleaded. "It's not like that at all."

"You want to take away what little faith I have!"

I felt like I was being scolded.

"Well, I assure you I know God! Who do you think brought us through all the tough times? And you tell me that I need to be saved?"

We were both crying. She was crying because her image of me was fractured. Her son had "gone over the edge." I was crying because I felt her slipping far away from me. I did not want that, but there was no way to fix the damage. My zeal had brought destruction. Our relationship could never be the same again.

She dried her eyes. "Let's do what we can to make the rest of your visit enjoyable. You keep your religion to yourself, and so will I."

I agreed reluctantly, and we hugged. Then she said, "Maybe we can talk again some time in a more rational way."

Phyllis and I drove back to California with our year-old son, the only redeeming value of our visit as far as Mom was concerned. I carried this heaviness for months about Mom. The Cult had clouded her mind.

One bright spot appeared. My sister, Joyce, told me that she had become a believer in Christ. She still lived at home with Mom and said that they had some religious discussions.

I wrote letters to Mom regularly, and she answered cordially as we traded news about her only grandson and her hometown. All of my letters ended with a verse of Scripture. I was hoping and praying that she would recognize how essential Jesus Christ is for salvation.

Phyllis was driving and I was reading the Bible one other time on vacation. I thought of Mom whenever I found a verse which might help her understand that she needed to be saved. But on this day, I discovered a verse which lifted the heaviness I felt for her, and allowed me to live in anticipation that some day she would understand and believe:

> My soul, wait silently for God alone, for my expectation is from Him. (Psalm 62:5)

I continued to pray for her and write letters, but with a new joy inside because I was expecting God to open her eyes, rather than depending on my own pleadings with her.

Seven years had passed, and I stopped to visit Mom on one of my trips to a conference. We were reminiscing in the same living room where her image of me was fractured that other time. My sudden change of pace surprised me, but it slipped out naturally. "Mom, there is nothing that would make Joyce and me happier than to know that someday we would be in heaven together with you forever."

No hysterics. Just a sigh, and a far away look in her eyes as she said, "That would make me happy, too, and I don't have the assurance that you both have."

"You can have the same assurance, Mom."

We prayed together, and she asked Christ to come into her life with salvation, forgiveness, and assurance. A happiness returned to her voice which had disappeared during that painful visit years before when I upset her with my zeal for her to be saved. This time we cried again, but with tears of joy, not fracture.

Joyce moved to take a job in Tacoma, and Mom moved out to a mobile home near us in California. Several years passed with precious memories as we got to include Mom in the family celebrations. She became ill with multiple sclerosis, but courageously faced an uncertain future, remaining as independent as possible. When she had a small stroke and needed 24-hour care, we transported her to an intermediate care facility. She died after a few days in her new surroundings.

Joyce and I conducted her funeral. It was a time to celebrate that she was home in heaven, having left her wheelchair for someone else to use. We described special memories of Mom in the presence of a dozen or so family members and friends. Although Mom did not have a diary, she often wrote down her thoughts and feelings. The high point of her memorial service was an excerpt from a note she wrote when the doctors thought she had cancer, before they diagnosed MS.

"God has a purpose for me, and I pray that I may never forget this, regardless of what the outcome of the surgery may be. If I am to face the sad battle against cancer, I pray that God will use me to bring a blessing to others. How? Only He can know, but surely He does nothing without a purpose. I know that Christ is my Savior, and I pray that He will use me in accordance with His good plan."

He only is my rock and my salvation; He is my defense;
I shall not be moved." (Psalm 62:6)

CHAPTER 31

FACING THE LIONS

One day the boss came into my cubicle. Before I had time to invite him, he had dropped onto my only visitor's chair and was leaning forward with his elbows on my table, holding his chin with both hands. "You know the forces you calculated for the safety valve pipes at Millstone?"

I certainly did remember! That had been one of those things I had never done before, and I had learned a lot. In fact, I had been able to devise a method to predict such forces, packaged it up in a report, and sent it to the customer. I remember praying a lot, too! That way I could leave the possibility of being wrong with the Lord, and go to sleep at night! "Sure, I remember. Why? Is something wrong?"

"The customer turned your calculation over to the NRC, as anticipated." The boss's voice began to sound strained. "The NRC had one of their consultants look it over...also as anticipated. But the customer decided to trust your calculations, and they have already installed braces and shock absorbers for the pipes."

"They probably should have waited until they got confirmation from the NRC," I mumbled. "But I am pretty sure the numbers we gave them are OK."

"I hope so," said the boss. "The NRC consultant claims that your numbers are too low by a factor of seven!"

"Seven!" Now I was leaning on the table. "Who is their consultant?"

"Have you ever heard of Norman Block? The famous gas dynamics expert? His father wrote the book on compressible flow! And I understand that Norman is following in his father's footsteps!"

I felt weak. I had used the famous book in school! If anyone would know how to do the calculation, Professor Block would---and I expect that his son would, too. "I'm not ready to just shrug this off," I said. "The customer trusted me! If my numbers are wrong, he's going to have to tear out a lot of concrete! He won't be happy!"

"You've got to go back and get this straightened out," the boss said, as he took a note out of his shirt pocket with lots of scribbling on it. "Here it is. They want you to meet with them and the NRC next Friday in Hartford. Mike will be the licensing guy going back with you."

That afternoon, I checked and double-checked my numbers. Even though I had prayed about them before they went out, I realized that prayer was no guarantee that I was right. Otherwise, I could pray before buying a lottery ticket, and win every time! But I did remember asking that God would use my work to accomplish His will both in my life, and in anyone else's who would be affected by what I did. As far as I could tell, my numbers were OK.

I had never traveled with Mike before. We arrived in Hartford after dark and drove to the hotel where we were to share a room. He went right to bed, and I sat at the desk making more checks on my calculations.

I heard something! Counting! It was Mike, lying there with a pillow over his head, counting in a whisper! He peeked out and saw me looking at him. "Don't mind me. I'm practicing self-hypnosis to get to sleep! Try it. You'll like it!"

He kept counting for 20 minutes. Every number he whispered, I could imagine a sheep jumping over a fence, although he insisted he was not counting sheep. It was useless to try to think with that going on. Whether it was working for him or not, his counting was making me tired. So I went to bed.

"Eight hundred and one... Eight hundred and two...."

I tried to pray. No use. I put the pillow over my head. Still no use. "How high can this guy count before he runs out of numbers?" I put my fingers into my ears. It worked! "Dear Lord, I hope that my calculations are right. Otherwise it will cast doubt on the credibility of both of us! Me, because I calculated them; You, because most people, including Mike here, know that I ask You to help me in all my analysis. But, Your plan is bigger than mine. If I'm wrong, use it however you want to, and get me through it, somehow."

I eased my fingers out of my ears. The counting had turned into snoring! I could tell this was going to be a wasted night, so I searched around in my head for scripture verses that might help. I seized on, "Fear not, for I am with you; Be not dismayed, for I am your God. I will strengthen you, Yes, I will help you, I will uphold you with My righteous right hand." (Isaiah 41:10) I was asleep before I finished the verse.

The next morning, Mike drove us downtown to the meeting. It was way up near the top floor in one of those tall buildings. We walked into a conference room where several customer executives met us and showed us to a place at a long table. "I'll sit closest to the door," Mike said to me, "in case I have to get out fast. That is, if the lions attack!"

I did not enjoy his sick attempt at humor. He was the licensing engineer. He had nothing to lose. I was on trial! Another verse..."I will never leave you nor forsake you." (Hebrews 13:5) I tried to breathe deeply.

NRC officials filed in, like umpires taking the field before the game. They were followed by a multitude of other customer personnel, consultants, and finally Norman Block! He sat directly across from me. He and I were supposed to fight it out like two pit bulls in a hole until somebody won! The table was the playing field! The stakes were high! I imagined that the people now occupying chairs that lined the surrounding wall were placing bets on the outcome! Norman Block began to speak, and the room got quiet.

"I reviewed the GE calculations done by Moody again last night, and discovered that the predicted forces actually are correct. They are not too low by a factor of seven as I originally suspected."

Silence. Nobody spoke. Nobody breathed. Nobody moved. VP's began to exchange glances. This meeting was costing them over $20,000 to get everyone there! Still, it was a small price to pay, compared to what it would have cost if my numbers had been wrong! I think one VP suddenly realized this and said with a smile, "Well, then! I guess we can all go home!"

Some people in the room looked disappointed. They had come to see bloodshed, and the game had been forfeited! Norman Block managed to disappear, almost like there was a trap door! We got an earlier flight home.

There have been other false alarms since then. I have imagined myself dead and buried over some of them that amounted to nothing. I realized again that God has given me the opportunity and ability to make specialized calculations, and He can take it all away whenever He wants to. But, when our life is hidden with Christ in God, it really doesn't matter.

Set your mind on things above, not on things on the earth. For you died, and your life is hidden with Christ in God.
(Colossians 3:2, 3)

CHAPTER 32

THE GOOD GUY AND THE VILLAIN

Phyllis and I could say that we have a "story-book marriage" with exciting plots, subplots, and happy outcomes at the end of most chapters. There have been good guys and villains, too. But how could this woman who exceeded my hopes and dreams, a matchless gift from God, turn out to be the villain in one of the chapters?

Money, or rather the lack of it, had a lot to do with our problems in one case; but the same problems could have been caused by other things like interference from in-laws, changing jobs, moving to another city, social obligations, raising children, or just about anything where people can have different views. I don't think I ever met a married couple who could not use more money. Every time I got a raise, it took Phyllis and me about fifteen minutes to go from feelings of happy anticipation to frustration. That's because by the time the boss called me in to give me the good news, we already had a list of things we wanted, which outpaced the amount of the raise.

"Now we can get this and that...but if we want to do that and this...then we can't have that and that and this and this...and by the time they take out taxes...!" FRUSTRATION!

The list of wants continued to grow. Reasonable wants. Things that other families like us were able to get. And even though the frustration increased, we decided, "No matter what happens, we want to put the Lord first in our finances." After all, everything we had came from Him. But that did not help our frustration. I tried to accept the fact that life is unfair, even the way wealth is distributed among our friends at Church.

Enter the almighty credit card! This had to be God's answer to frustration, we reasoned! The piece of plastic made it possible to go into a store and to come out carrying the thing that would make us happy—without having the money at the time!

My optimistic approach made it easy for me to justify. "As long as we are faithful to God in giving, He will provide." During this time, I kept my rigid practice of writing the church check as soon as I came home every payday. Then Phyllis wrote all the other checks, trying to pay our bills like she did when she was working to put me through school. But she did not share my optimism when she tried to write checks to cover our increasing credit card debt. I was doing my part. I brought home a paycheck every month, and Phyllis was stretching it as far as she could, often making minimum payments. I didn't notice the gradual change that was taking place in her. Over a period of several years, she became more quiet. She stopped humming tunes or singing songs around the house. We used to laugh a lot together. Now there seemed to be hardly anything to laugh about any more.

I thought it was her. Women are moody by nature, I reasoned, and no man alive fully understands them. We had three sons by then, and I wondered if her decline was an early symptom of menopause! I did all the right things like praying, leading family devotions, taking the family to church and Sunday school, as well as providing food, housing, and clothing. Any problems could not have been traceable to me. Neither could we blame the kids. There was only one other person to blame, and I was too kind to say anything to her about her apparent lack of financial ability.

We were taking our son, Paul, for weekly counseling at this time because of problems he had. The counselor eventually wanted to interview all of us together to see how we related to each other. There I sat in his office under protest, not in agreement that we should be spending money to get Paul straightened out when we could pray instead. Then came the jolt that I needed. It hurts when someone else points out your faults, especially when you think you have none! But you remember it. How stupid I had been! How blind!

The counselor had asked us how we felt about things—things we did, how we did them, feelings we had about each other and how we accepted each other. He turned to me. "Fred," he began, "you have to protect Phyllis more than you are."

"Protect her?" I thought. "I do! I provide! I lead family devotions! I pray! Besides that, I am kind. I treat her with respect. How can I protect her more than that?" I did not recognize this discussion as an answer to my prayers.

He explained a problem I had not identified. Phyllis saw me as the "good guy"--working hard and bringing the money home. She saw herself as the "villain," giving it all away to our creditors, never having quite enough left over. She was blaming herself for our financial woes.

"You should pay the bills in your family, Fred," he continued. "You should protect Phyllis from this frustration that she is not surviving emotionally. You must let her be the wife and mother God called her to be. As far as I can see, He did not call her to be your bookkeeper."

"That's too simple," I thought. The counselor could see that I was resisting the idea.

"If you do it, Fred, I will cut your bill in half." He really believed in his prescription!

I did not trust his advice at first, but we had already paid for many sessions, so I tried it. The results were astounding! Phyllis began to hum tunes and sing songs again as she kept house. She was happy like she had been several years before. She would even sit down at the table to watch me sweat over paying the bills. "How's it going?" she would ask. Together we added and subtracted numbers, balancing the checkbook. We actually began to enjoy this sadistic ritual! We joked and laughed when the checkbook balance was negative, and I had to redistribute the money among the creditors. We were both participating now, but the responsibility of protection was on me where it belonged.

So what is a negative balance when the humming and singing happy tunes has come back into a marriage?

> *These you ought to have done, without leaving the others undone. (Matthew 23:23)*

<u>Footnote</u>: This episode only describes how it was in our family. Every family is different. Some women should manage the finances because they can do it better than their husbands. Also, the credit card trap can increase the grip of financial stress on any marriage, and needs to be controlled. I think that the principle thing here is that a husband should be sensitive when any part of family life creates unreasonable stress on his wife that could be relieved by his greater participation in that responsibility.

CHAPTER 33

HELPLESS HAVOC

We began to notice that something was wrong with Paul, our third son. He suddenly began to lose weight at 27 years of age, and his already slender frame took on a malnourished appearance. Since we saw him once a week on Sundays when he came over after church, his weight loss was more dramatic. His brothers expressed their love and concern by referring to him as Paul, the anorexic-bulimic! It was OK, though; He had equally fond nicknames for them.

Paul had taken the jump to independence with a job at Radio Shack, and he was renting a house across town with two other young men. He stepped on his bathroom scale every day, and although he had a good appetite, he was still losing no matter how much he ate! Some of his heavier friends begged him to tell his secret for losing weight, but since he did not know the secret himself, he could not help them.

The increasing concern prompted an appointment with the doctor, who did some tests. When he could not diagnose the problem, he sent Paul to a specialist, and I began to think that this might be no ordinary problem. I remembered that one of the danger signals of cancer is unexplained weight loss! That raised my concern to the point of worry! I wanted the problem fixed as much as he did. But worry had come before, and by now I knew that this was a call to prayer...the thing we usually do when nothing else works!

We enlisted some close friends to pray for Paul during this period, but I knew that no one on earth could care as much as I did. I felt that I bore the greatest responsibility to Paul, so I determined to pray for him as though his well-being depended exclusively on my prayers. This situation motivated me to let out all the theological stops...but how do you pray effectively? How do you pray so that God answers? What kind of praying focuses all of heaven's power on your object of concern? I wanted to ask God to heal Paul, but my asking had to be in a way that He would answer. There had to be such a way to pray, because James wrote:

> *The effective, fervent prayer of a righteous man avails much. (James 5:16)*

I had to discover what made prayer effective. I already was praying fervently!

I found instruction for effective prayer in the Bible.

> *If I regard iniquity in my heart, the Lord will not hear. (Psalm 66:18)*

That meant that I had to be clean before I asked God. I got on my knees. I asked God to show me anything wrong in my attitudes toward sin. More than any other time in my life, I wanted to be totally clean before God. No dirt. Not even a speck of dust!

> *Purge me with hyssop, and I shall be clean; Wash me and I shall be whiter than snow. (Psalm 51:7)*

Now I could focus on Him. The prominence of everything else diminished.

> *Delight yourself also in the Lord, And He shall give you the desires of your heart. (Psalm 37:4)*

What I knew about God and His work became vivid in my mind. The creation of all from nothing. His everlastingness. His deliverance of Israel at the Red Sea. His miraculous birth in a stable. His hand reaching out to touch the leper. The nails in His hands and feet. His rising from the dead. The scars He bears that we might live with Him forever. His promised presence with us here to comfort, teach, guide.

I had gotten on my knees to ask God to heal Paul. But now I could not ask for healing! I realized that as strange as it might seem, a prayer for healing might have restricted what God could do! What I finally did ask was not in my plan:

"God, I want to pray as if I'm the only one praying about this—as if anything you do depends on my prayer. I know that you have a purpose for allowing this undiagnosed condition to come into Paul's life. Help him to know it, too, and help him to recognize your special touch on his life. Today, I want you to be seen in this by all of us, and others who may be watching. Show your power in any way that will bring joy to yourself. If you have joy, would you give us anything less? If your perfect plan includes Paul getting sicker and possibly dying an untimely death, I know that you would welcome him home to heaven, and you would also carry us through. I want you to be glorified. If you can be glorified in his healing, whether by miracle or medicine, let it be. Just give us the strength to bear up, and let us share your purpose, even though we see things through a dark glass."

I had read about "the peace of God, which surpasses all understanding," (Philippians 4:7). By the time I stood up again, He had given me that peace.

Paul went through another battery of tests by the "gut doctor specialist." I went with him for one of the tests. The specialist eased a long, black fiber-optic, illuminated tube down his throat to look at the inside of his stomach. Paul was awake, but they gave him something to numb his throat so he wouldn't gag. The doctor let me have a look after I promised not to pass out. Fascinating! Pink, wrinkled stomach walls spiraling down to a dark cavern, which turned out to be the duodenum. "Everything looks normal," the doctor remarked.

When he was extracting the tube, he slowly observed the walls of Paul's esophagus. "Wait a minute!" he exclaimed. "I think I have found a problem!" The doctor took a couple of tissue samples, and told us to come to his office next week. "If this is what I think, we can treat it." That's all he would say.

Naturally, Phyllis and I accompanied Paul to the specialist's office. "Crohn's disease," he said.

"Whose disease?" I asked.

We had never heard of Crohn's disease. It is an autoimmune condition where intestinal tissue attacks itself, thinking it is going after an infection. The result is inflammation of the intestinal walls, which limits the ability to absorb nutrients. That explained the weight loss!

"It's incurable," said the doctor, "but treatable with steroids and other medicines." Paul began treatment with frequent doses of Prednisone, and began to gain weight. We learned that a lot of people, including celebrities, suffer from Crohn's disease, and manage to live nearly normal lives. I was overflowing with thanksgiving to God when we left the office.

A few weeks later, I was at my desk wondering how I could meet all my work commitments. Several things were coming due, and if I failed to provide my part of the calculations, the projects would be in jeopardy. I was fretting about how I always managed to consent to schedules which all came due at the same time, when the phone rang. It was Paul. "I'm at home. Please come quick. Don't ask questions, just come!"

"I'm leaving now!" I assured him. Suddenly none of my deadlines mattered. I was out the door and breaking the speed limits all the way to his house.

When I pulled into his driveway, Paul came out of the front door, carrying a plastic bucket. His face was white. "My gut! It hurts so bad! I called the doctor, and he said to get to his office as quick as I could." He groaned all the way.

The doctor performed a quick examination, pausing only as Paul doubled over with his face in the bucket. He snatched up the phone to call the hospital. "I don't care if you have to put him in the hall! I want him there now! His intestine may have perforated!" We learned later that if Crohn's inflammation gets too severe, it can actually cause the intestines to perforate and spill into the abdomen, causing peritonitis which can be fatal.

X-rays showed no perforation, but Paul's pain continued in growing intensity. He was put in a bed, while his doctor conferred with several others about the best course of attack. Even during the flurry of hospital activity and Paul's agonizing pain, I believed that this was part of God's answer to my prayers. I sensed the quiet assurance God gives by the inner whisper, "You can trust Me." I prayed that God would relieve Paul's pain, as I helplessly watched him writhe on the bed.

I had called Phyllis at her job to tell her we were at the hospital, but not to worry; things would be okay. Of course, she came anyway, and the minute she walked into the room, things got better. She stroked Paul's head tenderly, and his groaning subsided.

The doctors decided to explore; and the surgery would be in about an hour. We called the rest of the family, and Paul's brothers arrived before surgery.

"Is this the anorexic-bulimic ward?" his oldest brother asked as he stepped up to the bed. Paul smiled for the first time that day.

My thankfulness overflowed quietly. "Thank you, God, for such a gross family!" They laughed and joked in Paul's presence to cheer him up until the orderly came with a roller bed to take Paul down to surgery.

The doctor came out after an hour or so. "Everything went well. He's fine. We took out a foot of his small intestine, which was badly inflamed. We'll have the lab study it to tell us the extent of his condition. He'll be able to recuperate at home in a few days." The doctor turned to go back to the operating room. "We also took out his appendix so that if he ever has trouble again, we can discount appendicitis."

"I suppose that costs more?" I mumbled happily, but he didn't hear me.

Paul recovered quickly and was back to a normal routine in two months. He discovered that Prednisone worked well if he started with a high dose when he had pain from inflammation, and then worked down. Prior to surgery, he was taking too small a dose, "chasing" the inflammation, but never catching it.

I have been amazed at his attitude. No bitterness. No feeling that God has treated him unfairly. It came out one night at a Crohn's and Colitis support group meeting I attended with him. Someone asked him, "How do you cope with this condition?"

Paul said that he had *two* answers, and he offered both. The first was for nonreligious people. "I figure, if I get mad or upset, it just aggravates the condition, so I accept it and get on the best I can. If I have a bad day, I know that tomorrow probably will be better."

The second answer? "I believe that God has a purpose for this, and I am content to let Him work out His plan in my life. I also have a very supportive family."

God has shown His power to all of us through Paul's condition. When he has had flare-ups, he asks us to pray. He lives each day in high expectancy that God has some things in store for him which are new and exciting.

I have no doubt that God has answered my fervent prayer. He is wonderfully glorified in Paul's life.

> *Be anxious for nothing, but in everything by prayer and supplication, with thanksgiving, let your requests be made known to God; and the peace of God, which surpasses all understanding, will guard your hearts and minds through Christ Jesus.*
>
> *(Philippians 4:6, 7)*

CHAPTER 34

BLAMED

"Whistleblower!" I did not know what the name meant, but comments in the hallway made it sound like a business opportunity for us. A large part of our business thrived on helping electric utilities to solve problems so that their nuclear reactors could continue generating power. Someone at one of the utilities suspected a problem with a measurement device used in the reactors. He was proclaiming his concern throughout the industry. The reason he was "blowing the whistle," he said, was that no one took him seriously.

Yes, there was a problem. No, it was not a safety concern, but it would have to be fixed. The Nuclear Regulatory Commission (NRC) had directed all utilities to fix the problem, and to submit a plan describing how they were going to do it within a year.

The nice thing about the problem was that there was no culprit. The problem existed for reasons that no engineer could have foreseen. No lawsuits. No threatening telephone calls to company vice presidents. Nobody to blame. A time limit meant no foot-dragging. Therefore, everybody involved in the nuclear industry was on the same side with the same battle cry, "Let's get it fixed!" Of course, business motives went hand-in-hand with the many organizations, who were now competing for the high stakes involved.

The reason I got involved was to provide an analysis which would be useful in determining how to fix the problem. It helps to know the physical reason a problem exists before you try to fix it. Otherwise, you can fix a problem that doesn't exist, and end up with worse problems than you would have if you did not fix anything at all. Besides, the exact cause of this problem was not fully understood, and needed analysis to help explain it.

I saw this as an interesting technical problem. The company saw it as an urgent opportunity to send out "how-we-can-help-you-fix-it" proposals to the utilities. The problem had to be fixed on the first try during a reactor shutdown for normal maintenance. Otherwise, it could cause an unscheduled shutdown, costing the utility up to a million dollars a day. The problem became serious from the standpoint of high costs to the utilities if the "fix" was bungled. We were counting on the fact that utilities often hired outside organizations to solve problems with serious financial implications. This problem was one of those. Besides, they liked large companies with many resources so that if anything went wrong, they could sue. Therefore, we were a front-runner for this business opportunity.

I finished the analysis and asked God for guidance in making the right predictions. Then I sent it on to the business strategy group, who sent out the proposals. The price was high, but we were the experts who would be taking a financial risk. We would defend it, and we would guarantee results. Soon, I joined the sales team at the airport, and we were on our way to a meeting with all the utilities.

Everyone seemed to enjoy the trip, except one person: the project manager. He just peered out of the window with a worried expression on his face. He was the one charged with keeping the job on schedule without cost overruns. We did not even have the job yet! When we were about halfway to the east coast, someone made the mistake of asking him how he was doing. "The boss intercepted me on the way out," he began. "He said it was unacceptable to come back without a contract to fix the problem for all the utilities." A chill settled on the team.

The rest of the flight was like a voyage to a funeral. I could sense what other team members were feeling. It was no longer a mission to make a first class presentation, and answer questions to *win* a contract; instead, it had become a mission to "come back with a contract, no matter what!"

This was no problem for God, I reminded myself, even though the boss's demands were not rational. I prayed, anyway. I was supposed to present the analysis. I wanted my efforts to contribute to the hard work of the other team members to make it a successful trip. I wanted to be like Jacob, whose uncle said, "I have learned by experience that the Lord has blessed me for your sake." (Genesis 30:27) I wanted the other team members to be able to say that of me.

I made the presentation the next morning. I described my analysis, just like class time at the University with a few differences. The audience was mostly men, older than the average undergraduate student. They were dressed in business suits, rather than grubby shirts and jeans. Neither was their attitude one of, "Please tell us more so that we can make our mark in the world as engineers." Instead, their attitude seemed to be a confrontational, "We dare you to convince us of anything!" The high-tech conference room was pervaded by a "wolfpack" atmosphere, and I perceived that if one of them went on the attack, the others would be close behind. It had happened to one of the earlier contenders who had dared to make some reckless claims he could not defend.

There was comfort knowing that if any of them decided to attack what I said, they would be attacking the laws of Newton, Fourier, and Fick, all famous scientists of historical renown, whose material I had used in my analysis. The fact remained that this audience was composed of those who would decide who got the contract.

Surprisingly, a few of them nodded their heads in approval during my presentation and seemed to appreciate my simple explanation, especially since I followed another contender who overwhelmed them with stacks of computer output and a complicated discussion. They asked a few questions of such a depth that I knew they had been listening carefully to what I said.

Several more contenders made presentations, and the utility representatives then met in a closed session. Toward the end of the day, it was announced that the contract would be awarded to one of the small companies! The solemnity of our team was like you would expect in a courtroom when the death sentence has been pronounced. No reasons were offered, but they would be transmitted within a few days. There was no appeal. No negotiating. Neither was there any celebrating on the trip home.

I came to work the next day with the rest of the team. We all hoped that our homecoming would have low visibility, since we had failed to win the multi-million dollar business opportunity. A relatively small company had outdone a Fortune 500 company! Bambi had trampled Gargantua! We knew that our price was high, but everyone was surprised to learn that price was a major reason we did not get the contract! Nobody lost his job. We did what most people do when they are defeated--we bandaged up our wounds and got on with business, since there were other projects that would keep us alive for a while.

This was the first year of voice mail! You could record a message, and send it to one or more people. Some managers had lists for general messages, and I was on several lists. That is why

I accidentally received a message which I was not supposed to hear. The conversation was between two bosses. One was demanding to know why we lost the contract. "We never should have lost this one! Even though the utilities say we were too high-priced, I doubt that money was the problem. They have too much at stake. What do you think the *real* reason is?"

The other boss answered, "I guess Fred was just not up to his usual level of performance. He did not convince them that we knew how to solve the problem."

When I heard that, I started to say something in my defense, before I realized that the voices I was listening to were recorded on voice mail! I had given one of my best presentations ever. The audience understood it. Now I was being blamed for losing the contract, even though the boss was too "polite" to tell me directly. "Oh, God," I moaned. "No! No! No! No! Don't let them think that! Neither one of them was there in the room during my presentation! They do not want to believe that we priced ourselves out of a contract! They are looking for someone to blame. I can't defend myself! I wasn't even supposed to hear their self-protecting conversation!" A feeling that I had failed our team began to come over me. That made me feel even worse. "Maybe they are right! God, what should I do? I prayed that you would help me make our team successful. I wanted to 'bless' them, just because I am yours. I wasn't supposed to hear that message. Should I go on being my usual cheery self? I can't pretend I did not hear it. I feel like I have been steamrolled!"

Peace! It came in a beautiful, welcome wave!"

If God is for us, who can be against us? (Romans 8:31)

I acknowledged, "I don't have to hang on to my reputation. God gave it to me in the first place, and He can take it away whenever He wants to. I know that He will never leave or forsake me. That's enough."

I slept. No tossing and turning or other distress, although I did not like to be blamed for something that was out of my control. But God was sovereign. None of this would have upset Him.

A few days passed, and a letter arrived on the boss's desk from the utilities. It was a detailed list of reasons for awarding the contract to the small company. Our proposal was indeed too expensive, but the letter went on to say that they liked my analysis, and they were willing to pay an hourly rate for me to be a consultant to the small company which had won the contract:

"We wish to contract for the services of Fred Moody, to provide his analysis of the problem in a form which can be employed in the computer program developed by (the small company) to whom the contract is awarded."

When I saw the letter, I went to my desk. "Thanks! You knew this from the beginning!"

It took my management *five minutes* to decide that they would not sell my services for "peanuts" in place of a possible multi-million dollar contract. It did not matter. God had turned blame into blessing.

> *Fear not, for I am with you; Be not dismayed, for I am your God. I will strengthen you, yes, I will help you, I will uphold you with My righteous right hand.*
> *(Isaiah 41:10)*

CHAPTER 35

SMALL THINGS THAT COUNT

"I'll show you how to take care of him," Dave said to his younger brother, Paul, who had just described how some bully had picked on him at school.

"Yeah, I know that kid," John said. "He thinks he's tough, but if you don't act scared, he's just a wimp!"

Family support! Most of the time, Dave and John were chief antagonists to Paul, but when Paul got picked on, both of his older brothers came to his rescue! Conversations like this usually happened during our evening family devotions, when we gathered in the living room.

I don't know where the idea of family devotions came from, but we held them from the time our first son, Dave, was still on a bottle. I would round up however many sons we had at the time, amidst protests. My sons tell me that when it was time for devotions, any other activity ceased to have priority. "You've been in that bathroom for half an hour. You've got 20 seconds to get out here!" I don't remember being that crude, but they say I was. Other activities, like a game of hide-and-seek in the front yard, had to stop immediately, even if one of them had found the perfect hiding place. TV programs were shut down in the midst of the most exciting part! That's what they tell me. I think they exaggerate!

We gathered in a family circle, some on the couch, one in the stuffed chair, one or two on the floor, Dave usually on his rocking horse. We sang some of the kid songs from Sunday School, with a few gospel hymns that we knew. All the while, Dave rocked, and Phyllis stroked the back, or leg, or head of one of the other boys. When we had sung a few songs, I read and tried to explain a chapter from the big family Bible we bought from a friend for $3.00 a month over one year! We still have that Bible, with its discolored page, caused by John's revenge one evening. He says that I insisted he was not too sick to sit on my lap during devotions. He proved that I was wrong by throwing up all over Numbers, Chapter 26! (So, I missed a diagnosis!)

Everyone had a chance to tell what was going on in his/her life after we finished the chapter. Then each of us prayed, while Dave continued to rock on his horse. I checked; He rocked with closed eyes when we were praying!

One night, we had some peculiar house guests, who gladly joined us for devotions. One of them took his turn to pray, "Dear Lord, please forgive us for being so irreverent during our devotions!" No doubt, he was making a reference to Dave on his rocking horse. We never invited him to join us again for our exercise in irreverence! He had serious problems of his own, like thinking that he did not have to pay his gasoline credit card because God wanted him to proclaim judgment against the greedy petroleum industry.

Whether we were irreverent or not, God blessed us and bonded us close together during family devotions. Our sons grew, and the rocking horse died, but devotions survived. Sometimes a playmate or two joined us during devotions. They usually were quiet, and not too judgmental. One frequent guest was Cameron, Dave's inseparable friend. He often came to Sunday School with Dave, too. Cameron had a sister, Kim. I remember her joining us for devotions once or twice. She did not say a word, but just sat there and watched.

One day during high school years, we learned that Kim was in the hospital from a drug overdose! No one had realized that she was taking drugs! Phyllis went to visit her. She prayed with Kim before leaving the hospital. Kim recovered, and soon moved out on her own. That was about 15 years ago.

Last year, a letter arrived at our house. It was from Kim. She reintroduced herself, "in case we forgot who she was." Then she recounted the times she had joined us for family devotions, which stirred something deep inside her. She remembered Mrs. Moody's visit when she was in the hospital, and it meant a lot to her. She thought we would like to know that God had used these things in her life, and that she had recently accepted Jesus Christ as her Savior. Her husband also had trusted in Christ, and was undergoing a successful drug rehabilitation program! They had joined a Bible-teaching church in Aptos, California, and were growing in their faith. They also had two children, and she said they would like to get together for a visit with us!

It was a rainy Sunday afternoon when we took Kim and her family out to a restaurant for lunch. We talked about the growing up years, how the Lord works through the small things, and how He gives strength to overcome problems. Her husband shared his warm appreciation for how God was working in his life to help him become the man of God that he wants to be for his family. Phyllis and I drove home with a lump of joy in our throats for the way God can salvage families, and show them what it means to live for Him.

Sometimes God peels back the curtain to show us that He can use the small things in our lives to touch someone for Himself. Like a brief hospital visit, or inviting a quiet, young girl to stay while we held "irreverent" family devotions!

> *But God has chosen the foolish things of the world to put to shame the wise, and God has chosen the weak things of the world to put to shame the things which are mighty; and the base things of the world and the things which are despised God has chosen, and the things which are not, to bring to nothing the things that are, that no flesh should glory in His presence. (I Corinthians 1:27-29)*

CHAPTER 36

DIAMOND IN THE ROUGH?

I had parked my car and was walking the last two blocks to the campus, on my way to teach an early afternoon class. The last block takes me through a neighborhood that has a variety of ethnic shops, festive colors, people, and food aromas. It is a melting pot with almost every "tribe and nation" represented.

This neighborhood also abounds with economic extremes. I have seen the well-dressed businessmen in wrinkle-free suits, crossing paths with the homeless, who push shopping carts full of aluminum cans and a few belongings. Superimpose on this background young men and women with backpacks, dressed in their grubbies, fit for the classroom. Some are walking, some ride bicycles, and some move about in wheelchairs. Occasionally, I see one crossing the street with a guide dog. I wear a suit and tie, and carry a briefcase!

It is not my desire to stand out in the crowd. I just don't want anyone to confuse me with the students! I don't wear a sign that says, "Adjunct Professor," but by dressing like I was going to the office, I reduce the probability of mistaken identity!

Hundreds of students have gone through my classes in 24 years of teaching. I get letters, or phone calls from some of them, and occasionally, someone with a familiar face will approach me in a crowd to remind me that they took a class from me. If the face is smiling, I know he/she must have gotten a good grade. One of the most rewarding things about teaching is that some students tell me that I made a positive difference in their lives.

I had walked across Santa Clara Street and was starting down the last block to school, when I heard someone call, "Mr. Professor! Mr. Professor!" I thought that in the midst of this multi-cultural environment there probably were not more than a couple of professors, and that narrowed down the possibility that someone was calling to me!

"Mr. Professor!" I was right. A man was coming across the street toward me. He was limping, holding one hand on his leg, and attempting to run! He was a tall, slender black man in his thirties, wearing a wrinkled sports coat, open shirt with stains on it, a dirty pair of pants, and sandals. He was smiling. I had stopped walking and was trying to remember if he ever had been in one of my classes.

"Mr. Professor!" He stepped up onto the curb and extended his hand. Up close, he was much taller than he had appeared at first, and I had to look up at him while I shook his hand. I still was not sure if he was a former student, but he continued to smile. Almost every other front tooth was missing. "You are a professor, aren't you?" He studied me.

"How did you know? Oh, I bet my necktie gave me away! Yes, part-time." The smell of wine was strong. His eyes were bloodshot, and he was still shaking my hand.

The smile on his face collapsed into a frown. His words became direct. "Well, I'm mad. I'm hungry. And I need a dollar and ninety seven cents!"

I studied him for a minute while I thought, "Extortion!" When he saw that I needed to reach into my pocket, he let loose of my hand. My other hand was hanging onto my briefcase. "I'm sorry, I don't have the exact change. Will you take $2.00?"

The smile came back to his face. It occurred to me that somewhere in the plan of God, I had been spared from the plight of this man, who was having some difficulty slipping the $2.00 into his partly torn shirt pocket. "Be sure to spend it on food," I said.

"Oh! I just smell like this because somebody threw a bottle of wine on me!"

I thought of another time when the Apostle Peter said to a beggar, "Silver and gold I do not have, but what I do have I give to you: In the name of Jesus Christ of Nazareth, rise up and walk." (Acts 3:6) Maybe this meeting on the street was a Divine appointment, and the $2.00 was a small price to pay for an opportunity to tell him how Christ had changed my life. I was too slow, however. He had turned and was almost rounding the corner. I tried to justify myself by reasoning that he probably had been preached to a lot of times, anyway. But I had to say something...anything! I called after him, "It's in the name of Jesus."

He whirled around, and his face broke into a look of surprise. "Jesus? Did you say Jesus?" For an instant, all barriers vanished between a street person and a college professor, standing ten feet apart on a downtown sidewalk. It was obvious to me that both of our lives had been changed by the single, most important Name known to man. He reached into his shirt pocket and pulled out a tattered New Testament. "I know Him! God bless you, brother!" He came over and shook my hand again, and then he disappeared around the corner.

I walked the last block to class. "Brother?"

I could have given him more! Maybe a few words that would have encouraged him and helped him. I wished that I had told him, "Christ didn't die so that you have to live like this." But I hadn't. Maybe next time.

Besides, he did not want advice. He only wanted $1.97.

Lord, when did we see You hungry and feed You? And the King will answer and say to them, 'Assuredly, I say to you, insomuch as you did it to one of the least of these My brethren, you did it to Me.' (Matthew 25:37, 40)

CHAPTER 37

TABLOID TRAPS

"Man abducted by aliens."

"Dead woman revived on embalming table. Says, 'It was beautiful over there! I did not want to come back.'"

"Wear this charm and get everything you want in life!"

Page after page of the shocking! The unbelievable! Information you can't find in respectable newspapers. THE TABLOIDS! These undersized newspapers show up anywhere. They are dumped into the mainstream of the masses at newsstands, magazine racks, or check-out lines in stores. Used copies can be found in restaurants, phone booths, waiting rooms, airport lounges, on streetcars, trains, and in trash cans.

I discovered tabloids years ago in the barber shop. I was waiting my turn. One was on the chair next to me, so I picked it up and paged through it. I thought it was a collection of absurdities or some kind of joke newspaper, with articles and ads from fanciful writers, trying to outdo each other. It only took a few minutes for me to decide that a stinking can of garbage has more literary and redeeming social value than tabloids! However, people buy them. Worse, they read them! Even worse, they enjoy them! I still pick up a used copy now and then and absolve myself of guilt by muttering something like, "I can't believe people are so gross and gullible."

My only explanation for the amusement people find in these underground newspapers is that each of us is born with a "tabloid mind." It is exposed by a craving to read about the indiscretions of prominent people, the secret lives of superstars, and the absurd "truth" behind everyday headlines, including UFO's and the ongoing invasion by aliens among us. If those things are too far-fetched, we can turn to the advertisements and discover that we can send for special charms to attract money, fame, and members of the opposite sex! Even born-again Christians with a new nature and destiny from God are still afflicted by the unconverted old nature, which enjoys an occasional trip to the gutter of human depravity via the printed page.

I think that the tabloids take advantage of people who are bored with life, and need gossip, distortions, and outright lies to feed their fantasies. Believing a lie can be so enjoyable! Unbridled imagination can be great entertainment! Furthermore, we seem to have an inherent laziness which does not like to make the effort to find out the truth. We would rather be told about something outrageous and not have to verify it. That makes us vulnerable to the tabloids! A mind which does not inquire, verify, ask, and compare information is likely to become a tabloid mind.

A lot of us seem ready to assume the worst possible scenario about what we see. For example, an older man has dinner with a young woman at an exclusive restaurant. Someone with a tabloid mind sees them, assumes the worst without verification, and soon everybody knows that the old guy is cheating on his wife. It turns out that the young woman is his daughter, who is home between college semesters! The tabloid battle cry remains, "Tell just enough of what you see to set the stage, and let all the hungry imaginations fill in the rest!" That sells copies!

I sometimes let my mind fall into the tabloid mode. I wish that I did not. It is easy for me to supply missing facts when I see something questionable or incomplete. The only person I know about who can supply the missing facts and extract the truth every time is Perry Mason! Since the world has only one Perry Mason and a lot of people like myself, whose minds function occasionally in the tabloid mode, I try not to give anyone a reason to think the wrong thing.

I suppose I should be thankful for being able to shift gears to the tabloid mode. It helps me to sense what others might be thinking. Consequently, there are situations I try to avoid, even though it may seem ridiculous to some. For example, a lot of women take my engineering classes. Sometimes they want to discuss a homework problem with me. These students are not dirt-ugly boilermakers! They generally are smart, poised, well-presented young women, whom I would be pleased to have as younger sisters or even daughters, although one of them was old enough to have been my mother! (She got an "A" in the class.) However, I have what I think is a healthy paranoia when it comes to women students in general. I remember that in the Old Testament, Joseph was suddenly alone with Potiphar's wife in Egypt (Genesis 39). Although he ran away to avoid compromise and was innocent, lies and tabloid gullibility sent him to prison.

Not that I think women students are "out to get me", but even the most innocent activities can be misinterpreted, misrepresented, and bring permanent scars in this day of suspicion and hypersensitivity to exploitation issues. That is why I discuss school work with women students only when other students are around. The cafeteria, hallway, the department office, the library. Even though there is commotion, it is the good sound of people coming and going, while we plant ourselves in plain sight so that anyone with a tabloid mind won't have anything to publish.

The classroom is only one place that provides fodder for fantasies. The office is another. Many of my women students have become engineers, joining their sisters from other schools in an assault on a profession historically dominated by men. The ranks of women engineers have grown beyond most estimates, balancing the mix of men and women in many branches. Women engineers brighten up otherwise "ho-hum!" meetings, and usually the conversation is less vulgar when they are present. Also, perfume is better than stuffy air and coffee breath.

The mix of working men and women engineers (almost any profession could be substituted for engineering), sets the stage for tabloid potential. For instance, sometimes it is necessary for men and women to travel together to an out-of-town meeting. The travel agent may seat you together on the plane and accidentally make a single room reservation at the hotel for both travelers, having to work from a list of just first initials and last names. Also, many government employees are on a strict per-diem, which makes some travel planners think in the mode of doubling up people in hotel rooms to keep costs down! Unless the traveling team involves three or more people, a man and woman alone on a business trip can give way to compromising situations where one could be vulnerable to the temptations of the moment. I am paranoid about this, too.

Old fashioned? Yes. But my wife and I have been happily married to each other for over 40 years. Our relationship is built on TRUST.

I traveled with Kirk and Sabrina quite a few times during a two-year period to many national labs, power plants, and professional meetings. Three was a perfect number for this activity. Low cost, high benefit, no compromise. It was called "the road show," because we were proclaiming the ultra-tremendous features of the GE nuclear power plants. The company motive, of course, was to help outsiders view GE as the "vendor of choice" when it came to power. All three of us were married.

Sabrina was a hard driver who thrived on work! I doubt that she needed more than two hours of sleep at night. She was a unique feature of the "road show" because she was not only a woman, but a smart woman engineer. Kirk and I performed our part in the first half-hour of the presentation, and Sabrina did the last monologue.

Several times when the prospective audience discovered that a woman was on the program, chauvinist slobs came, sat smugly in the back of the room, and waited until she got well into her discussion before they "began the test." It usually started with an interruption. A hand would go up. Sabrina would acknowledge it. Then, the owner of the hand, obviously on a personal mission to rattle her, would ask the toughest question he could generate, sometimes ending with a sarcastic snarl. (Heaven help the one who interrupted her first!) His tone might imply that she was not addressing the important issues, and why should he waste his time listening to her? I have seen male engineers fold when confronted with such audience hostility. Not Sabrina! She would wax eloquent as she shot back something like, "I covered that in the first three minutes of my talk, if you had been listening." Then without hesitation, she would proceed, while the red-faced adversary usually cleared his throat and soon left the room as if he had something more important to do.

Sabrina taught me a vital lesson I shall always remember. We had just finished the "road show" and had returned to the hotel. Kirk and I accompanied Sabrina in the elevator on the way to her room to call the boss and tell him how it went. The elevator stopped at the sixth floor. Kirk stepped off, and Sabrina stayed on. "I want to drop this package off at my room first," he said. "Go ahead without me and I'll join you in a few minutes."

"Oh, oh!" I thought.

The elevator stopped at Sabrina's floor, and we both got off. She pulled the key out of her purse and opened the door of her room. I froze in the hallway! She was holding the door open, and I just stood there, trying to think of a nice way to stall until Kirk arrived. Then with unmistakable irritation, she said, "Come on in! We've got to call the boss before he goes home!"

I mumbled something about how I would rather wait until Kirk got there.

Then came the important lesson.

Sabrina turned, bolted into her room, and immediately returned with her suitcase. "Here, for Christ's sake!" She slammed the suitcase up against the door to hold it open, and stomped back inside to dial the phone.

What a brilliant solution!

PROP THE DOOR OPEN!

No sober person I know ever behaves in a questionable way with the door propped open! Even so, I managed to straddle the threshold in full view of the elevator until Kirk arrived.

Sabrina not only taught me one way to avoid tabloid potential by putting a suitcase, chair, or other heavy object against the door to prop it open, when the occasion comes suddenly, she also gave me the most profound reason for being paranoid (or especially careful) I could have vocalized.

"For Christ's sake!"

Abstain from every form of evil. (I Thessalonians 1:8)

CHAPTER 38

BROKEN HEARTS

My first broken heart came in high school. It involved a girl: Jenny. Maybe my heart was not really broken— but it was cracked!

Jenny had come to Aurora to spend the summer with her aunt and uncle. Her uncle owned an automobile dealership where my mother worked. He knew that my mother had a son in high school, and Jenny was bored because she did not know anyone her age in our town. Could I take her out to introduce her around so the summer would be fun? Since I had not met Jenny, how could I be sure that she did not resemble a line-backer for the Chicago Bears? I did not want to commit myself to becoming a personal escort for a lady sumo wrestler, so I said that I could take her to a barbecue on Friday. No promises of anything else after that.

I rang the doorbell, telling myself that I was ready for any-thing! This was like a blind date! The door opened, and there she stood! Dark, flashing eyes. Happy excitement in her voice. Perfume. Besides that, she had a driver's license and her uncle would let her use his car! That was the first date! By the time she went back to her home in Kansas City, we vowed to write to each other.

Weekly letters flew back and forth until November, and although I kept writing, she stopped! At first I thought she might have hurt her hand, in which case she could have at least dic-tated a post card with details of the mishap. Nothing came. I wrote asking, pleading, begging her to write. Was there someone else? Did she move? Was it bad breath or B.O.? Didn't she still like me? No answer. Mom blamed herself for my frustration, since she had volunteered me to be Jenny's escort in the first place.

When a few more weeks passed with no letters from Kansas City, Mom explained that Jenny's folks probably decided to put the kabosh on our friendship because Jenny was a Jew and I was a Gentile...and she was probably head over heels in love with me...and they didn't want her to give up her religion...and some-day marry outside her faith...and so forth! I discovered that mothers know how to comfort sons who have had a female break their hearts! I felt better. I also followed one of Mom's suggestions for my last letter to Jenny. It consisted of a red paper heart cut in two pieces to look broken, with the message, "Ouch!" I healed up in time for the Christmas holidays.

Guys and gals still break each other's hearts. That's a risk you take if you begin to really care about someone. One of my engineering students told me at the final exam that she was having trouble concentrating because her boyfriend had just broken her heart by dumping her! However, she got the highest score in the class! (I wouldn't dare draw a conclusion from that case.)

I saw another student, Garth, sitting on the floor in the hallway with his head down. He wasn't praying, either! I told him, "You look like you lost your last friend."

"It's worse than that," he confessed. "My heart just got broke! My girlfriend wants to break up! You know—she wants to date other guys "

I tried to sound like I had a lot of experience in this sort of thing, as I proceeded to give him a piece of fatherly wisdom. "Tell her that you realize she 'needs some space', and you want her to be happy, so you'll back off for a while. She'll soon discover how wonderful you are, and probably come back to you." I had his full attention. "A bird will perch on your hand, but if you hold its feet, it will struggle to get away. Once you release it, it may fly a circle or two, but then comes back to land on your hand!"

I knew he was not ready to be cheered up when he replied, "The bird probably will do something else on your hand!"

My experience with students and young professionals who share their hurts leads me to believe that most broken hearts are caused by broken relationships. One person rejects another who wants to be accepted. The one with the broken heart is the one who has been rejected. Divorce can be one of the most painful rejections. My mother's heart was broken when our dad divorced her for the other woman. My sister and I suffered from broken hearts when it finally became clear that he had divorced us, too! Rejects! Parents rejecting children, and children rejecting parents cause tears to flow. A symptom of broken hearts.

Hearts also can be broken when people suddenly realize they have done irreparable damage to someone they love. Or they reach out to someone they care about at the risk of further rejection, only to be rejected more cruelly than before. Or they see a son or daughter being rejected, and they cannot come to the rescue. Or they want to hold a special person close to assure them of love and acceptance, and the whereabouts of the person is unknown. The list does not stop.

A broken heart gives pain for a long time. Its symptoms are a heaviness in the middle of the chest, accompanied by an intense desire to see a relationship changed. Memories that once brought happiness now bring sadness, with an inner longing for a relationship to be restored. A broken heart can't be seen on the outside, and it can be understood only by those who have had theirs broken.

I observe people in a flurry of academic and business activities every day. They are caught up in crises that have to be resolved. They are hurrying on their way to meetings. They are rushing to the weekend getaway. They meet you going the opposite direction. Some smile, or laugh, or tell a funny story, or wish you well. Derail them by asking how things *really* are, and you may hear another side.

Here comes Roy, a retired engineer, with a warm smile and his usual cheery greeting. I ask how his son Mark is getting along with his degree in chemistry. I can see that tears are close to the surface. "Mark lost his last two jobs. He has become an alcoholic."

Ed returns after a long absence. "I just came back from burying my son. He took his own life." He tries to tell more, but the words won't come.

A little girl tells Santa Claus that all she wants for Christmas is a hug from her daddy. He's in jail.

Dick joins other men in a prayer group. He can hardly articulate his pain for a wayward daughter, who has not communicated for weeks. They don't know if she is living on the street, or dead, or what.

Larry and Nancy visit their son in prison every week. He is serving a life sentence.

A retired doctor, in the box during jury selection for a narcotics case, responds to a query from the defense lawyer. "Yes, I have first hand experience with drugs. My son is on them." His voice trembles. "He's out there, and I don't know where he is."

A mother anguishes, "My two sons have not spoken to each other for years."

A mom and dad ask, "What can we do? Our son needs help, and we can't reach him."

Broken hearts. People wishing they could change the circumstances. Powerless to help. Feeling the pain, which goes on and on.

Most of us want a broken heart to be fixed, and we keep wishing, hoping, and looking for remedies, while we go on hurting. Listening to ads for aspirin and other analgesics makes us think that pain of any kind is bad. However, the built-in capacity we have to experience pain does work for good, sometimes! Pain makes us careful about touching a hot stove. Pain helps us avoid slamming the car door on a person's hand. Pain can protect us, keep us from injury, and sometimes from death. What about the pain of a broken heart?

I was surprised to find nearly a thousand references to the *heart* in the Bible—not the muscle that pumps blood, but that part of us where we feel our emotions. When we are sad, or happy, or angry, we do not feel it in our heads. We feel it somewhere inside our chests, between the chin and navel! The heart! There are scriptural references which show that a broken heart gives its owner special access to God!

> *The Lord is near to those who have a broken heart, and saves such as have a contrite spirit. (Psalm 34:18)*

A broken heart can be offered up to Him as a precious sacrifice!

> *The sacrifices of God are a broken spirit, A broken and a contrite heart—These, O God, You will not despise. (Psalm 51:17)*

Although we may try a lot of over-the-counter products, God alone can ease the pain of a broken heart.

> *He heals the brokenhearted and binds up their wounds. (Psalm 147:3)*

A broken heart may compel a person to some action. In one instance, Paul had to write a letter to affirm his love for those who questioned it.

> *For out of much affliction and anguish of heart I wrote to you, with many tears, not that you should be grieved, but that you might know the love which I have so abundantly for you. (2 Corinthians 2:4)*

The pain in his heart drove him to keep telling the message of hope in Christ, with a willingness to die himself for those he especially loved, who were missing the life God intended for them.

I have great sorrow and continual grief in my heart. For I could wish that I myself were accursed from Christ for my brethren, my kinsmen according to the flesh, (Romans 9:2,3).

The pain, the longing, the intense desire in his heart, not unlike the way we may feel, compelled him to write again:

I make mention of you always in my prayers,
(Romans 1:9)

(I)..make mention of you in my prayers:" (Ephesians 1:15)

We..pray always for you. (Colossians 1:3)

Okay, Paul. We get the idea. A broken heart is an invitation to prayer. Accompanying tears are permitted, too, since they are precious to God, even from the machos!

You number my wanderings; Put my tears into Your bottle; Are they not in Your book? (Psalm 56:8)

Where do we take all this? What is practical? Some of us have discovered that God allows our hearts to break so that He can have more access to our lives. The pain is a reminder to drive us to prayer, day and night, casting ourselves on Him.

Casting all your care upon Him, for He cares for you.
(I Peter 5:7)

I once saw a pictoral sweat shirt hanging on a wall. It showed the end of a rugged wooden beam and a hand against it with the open palm facing outward. Two of the biggest, ugliest spikes I ever saw were driven through it, where the wrist joined the palm. Their heads were bent down in opposite directions. There were only two words:

LOVE HURTS

In case we forget, Jesus Christ, Our Savior knows all about broken hearts. No one ever suffered the ultimate rejection that He did.

He is despised and rejected by men, A Man of sorrows and acquainted with grief. (Isaiah 53:3)

For one moment of unspeakable anguish, even God rejected Him, while He took our sin upon Himself, and cried out,

My God, My God, why have You forsaken Me?
(Matthew 27:46)

It did not end there. His broken heart was a passage to joy, for it says of Him,

> *Who for the joy that was set before Him endured the cross, despising the shame, and has sat down at the right hand of the throne of God. (Hebrews 12:2)*

A broken heart is our invitation to come to Him, the One who says He is near. The One who understands. The One who is all we need.

CHAPTER 39

MARRIAGE—SURVIVING OR THRIVING?

"What is the toughest personal problem your students ever have to face?" I wanted to know because I work with university students.

A thoughtful look came over my friend, who is a popular professor at MIT. His answer surprised me. "One problem more than most others. It's not a death in the family like you might think. When someone dies, we send students home for a week, give them time to catch up in their courses, and generally get them back on their academic plan. The toughest problem comes when they learn that mom and dad are getting a divorce! Some students are devastated, and we may never get them back!"

The thought of divorce reopens a wound. I suffered for years after my dad divorced my mother for someone else. Technically, he divorced my sister and me, too. The pain still has not completely disappeared. We grew up feeling that something was wrong with us. Otherwise, he would have stayed. We were rejects in our own minds. If he had died, at least it would not have been our fault that he was gone. My friend was confirming that sometimes death is easier on the survivors than divorce!

I know of couples with strong marriages who were once on the verge of divorce. Because something happened, they have fallen more in love than ever. Now they have an itinerary which unfolds daily as they travel through life together making new discoveries. They reach their first, tenth, twenty-fifth, fortieth, fiftieth wedding anniversaries, happily anticipating the next year to come.

I also know of couples who have arrived at the later years, and have become the center of interest in beautiful sunsets for younger generations to see. Birthday parties in the dining room of the retirement home, with so many candles on the cake that they have to put the fire department on alert! Aged couples, shuffling along with sacks of groceries, holding onto each other. An elderly gentleman daily going to the convalescent hospital where he sits by the bed of his wife to hold her hand and assure her that he is still there. These "snapshots" show the world that a husband and wife can "love, honor, and cherish each other until this life is over."

My marriage to Phyllis has rolled through 40 years! Some of it has been surviving, and some of it thriving! We have survived disappointments, frustrations, unfulfilled expectations, and other hurts. We have thrived in the assurance of each other's unconditional love and acceptance. We were as naive as any young couple, with stars in our eyes, but we made some early promises to each other that we meant to keep, "..as long as we both shall live."

God continues to stretch us through the surviving times, which always end happily and make us stronger, showing that we have an unbeatable team of three—Himself, herself, and myself. Together we win! We cannot lose because we have instant access to His strength and wisdom.

> *Though one may be overpowered by another, two can withstand him. And a threefold cord is not quickly broken. (Ecclesiastes 5:16)*

Young couples seem surprised that we have been married to each other for so long. Others who know us admire what God has accomplished. So do we, when we consider the dysfunctional baggage I brought into our marriage, and Phyllis' complete inexperience in the care and feeding of a maladjusted young man like I was.

I am puzzled that no one ever asks me, "What is your secret of a long, happy marriage?" Come to think of it, I have never asked someone that question, either. I think we are afraid of asking such a question because it sounds like we are confessing ignorance. We've got this funny idea that a marriage, where two people live happily ever after, is something we are supposed to know how to do by instinct. But no one becomes a welder, electrician, surgeon, or a hundred other things by instinct. We don't even become a functioning individual without someone to show us how. We learn, we get experience, we watch, we ask. Then we tell others how easy it is! I believe that one reason many marriages develop trouble is that the couples *do not ask* those, whose lives demonstrate that they might have some answers! I also believe that I have a responsibility to speak out, even if no one does ask! Isn't that what professors are expected to do? We don't always know what we're talking about, but people listen, anyway!

It is amusing to me, adjunct professor at a local university, that even though we may be trained in some obscure subject like *statistical thermodynamics*, multitudes of trusting people consider us to be experts in everything! Because we have a Ph.D. after our names, we automatically have an audience! A university professor speaks about a controversial topic, and the media proclaims it for him, no matter how asinine his message is.

"University Professor says,

'New evidence that Goliath had a thyroid problem.' 'Sun will burn up in eight billion years, two billion years sooner than formerly predicted!'"

Who cares? Nevertheless, with luck the outrage pops up on the front page the day after he says it, and he has instant fame! Whatever he says doesn't have to be verified, as long as it sells copies! But let a truly wise man give a workable answer to one of life's problems, and, if he has no advanced degree, his words may go unnoticed!

When it comes to a happy, thriving marriage of 40+ years together, I feel like I owe the world an explanation. Some will want to hear it, and some will react as if it is a TV commercial--an excuse to do something else. Nevertheless, I have discovered FOUR PRINCIPLES that are too good to keep secret. None of the principles are new, but they should generate some ideas for a husband and wife who want their marriage to be better, no matter how good or bad it is now. All the principles have been within reach since the first Bible was printed! THESE ARE NOT THEORY. THESE ARE LIVING TRUTHS. THEY REALLY WORK!

That part of me which is engineer has taken these principles and organized them into four practical laws for a thriving marriage. The only way I can discuss these laws in a credible way is from the man's point of view. I think that wives will also appreciate these laws, and find ways to communicate them to their husbands...like wrapping up little notes in his sandwich, or sticking them on the mirror in the bathroom. Here they are:

LAW #1. CARING PROVIDES A PATH FOR THE LOVE OF
GOD TO FLOW BETWEEN TWO PEOPLE.

I can identify CARING in my marriage by a desire to GIVE whatever I can for the benefit of my wife. Knowing exactly what will benefit her is essential, or I may give the wrong thing! Sometimes she tells me, but if she doesn't, I have to find out. I have given her presents which she graciously accepted, but never was able to use! I gave her a "Quilt in a Day" kit once, with a six-hour class to go with it at a sewing shop. Then I discovered that she enjoys sewing as much as she enjoys getting dirt in her eye!

> *What man is there among you who, if his son asks for bread, will give him a stone? (Matthew 7:9)*

Caring can be measured by the time and effort we are willing to give because CARING INVOLVES GIVING, and GIVING INVOLVES GIVING UP. The only thing we can GIVE without GIVING UP is something we don't want in the first place, like a sack of garbage. But GIVING UP means putting someone else first.

One of the most gut-wrenching things to GIVE UP is our plans! My plans used to be so rigid that if I had to compromise in order to accommodate Phyllis's plans, I might go on an extended "pout." One evening, I began to learn the solidifying effect it could have on our marriage if I would be willing to GIVE UP. That meant changing my plans, or putting my plans on hold, or abandoning my plans altogether...just for her. I was a regular at midweek prayer meeting. It was my mark of "religious service." One time, Phyllis had cared for our sick baby all day. She had dark circles under her eyes by evening, but church came first, and I got into the car alone. Halfway to church, God interfered. "They need you worse at home." I did not hear a deep voice, but I knew that the message was from Him. I changed my plans. I'm glad I turned around and went back; that was the best thing I could have done! It meant a lot to our marriage. It told Phyllis something she did not hear very often during those early years: It said, "I care." The Lord has this to say about religious service and other responsibilities:

> *These you ought to have done, without leaving the others undone. (Luke 23:23)*

Care also is measured by little things that show we think about the other person when we are apart. Everyone likes to know that he/she is special to a significant other person. I am slow when it comes to realizing how important the little things can be. Frequent gifts...her favorite flowers or candy, earrings, perfume, anything I can buy, make, or even suggest with her in mind. (I have a friend who could not convince his wife that the push lawn-mower he bought for her birthday present was really for her benefit!)

Caring is shown by planning special times together. Phyllis still likes me to date her. Planned dates are great, but so are spontaneous dates, like the early years when I used to say, "Honey! Let's blow our life's savings on a movie tonight!" She appreciates anything I do that is designed with her in mind. A surprise...A party...A trip, or an event...Something planned just for her!

Caring also is shown by frequent personal contacts. I live in Silicon Valley. They make every device possible imaginable for storing and transmitting information, except spare human brains. Many of them can be used to show that we care. All we have to do is type in the e-mail address, or scribble a note and send it on the fax (risking that the wrong person might pick it up) or punch the numbers on a touchtone phone and talk to either a live person or an answering machine. We have no excuse for not communicating our care. With all of this capacity, I try to contact her on special occasions...or on days when I know she is having it rough...or just to hear her voice...or for no particular reason. She does the same for me.

Caring generates enthusiasm, instead of confrontational interrogation. This approach works wonders, even-though we may not always be in total agreement.

"I'll be glad to help you move furniture! Are you thinking 'room rearrangement' or a trip to the dump?" (The longer you are married, the more there is to move.)

"A new overstuffed chair? Let's go to the furniture store where WE can find something WE like. When WE do, we'll sit down in a nice restaurant and figure out which one of the kids we can sell to pay for it!"

"Let's discuss steps we can take to make this dream come true!"

"You invited whom over for dinner? Of course it's okay. I know that the TV station will be glad to postpone the Super Bowl so that I can watch it another time!"

Caring about the things she cares about is a way to care about her. It lets love flow.

> *He who is married cares about the things of the world—how he may please his wife. (I Corinthians 7:33)*

LAW #2. COMMUNICATING ALLOWS US TO DISCOVER
            WHAT WE CAN DO THAT WILL BENEFIT THE OTHER.

One year Phyllis and I gave ourselves the most important Christmas present ever. We still have it, and plan to keep it until either we wear out or it does. This thing caused our communication to jump at least 10 levels! It provides an environment where we dream a lot of wild dreams, make a lot of absurd plans, solve problems of our own and anybody else's, learn what is going on in each other's head, and discover ways to CARE more. It is a double rocking chair!

"Time out!" one of us will say during the evening. We will then pull ourselves away from whatever we are doing, and spend the next five to fifty minutes side-by-side. Lack of communication is impossible when we are in this rocker! One of us makes a comment; the other adds a thought. The chemistry often creates the unexpected! Plans, dreams, goals, solutions, vibrating expectancy, special celebrations, great vacations, superb weekends, fulfilling projects, and new endeavors we were afraid to attempt before have been born in that rocker! Sometimes even a confession about some way one of us has hurt the other comes out. Most of our "time outs" begin with profound statements, like:

"How was your day?"

"What's happening this weekend?"

"When are you going to call the roto-rooter?"

"This is what happened. What would you do?" "Do you remember when we..."

"Did you have garlic for lunch?"

"You say the airbag worked?"

Even if we are too tired to carry on much of a conversation, we are still together side by side and available to each other, in case one of us has local news...or needs a sounding board...or has a heavy thing to discuss.

A double rocker is not essential for communication. Anyplace works where we can have access to each other's attention. Hypnotized in front of the TV usually doesn't encourage communication, even though we are together. Real communication begins when we turn the TV off!

We never HAVE time for communication. We MAKE time, and that is when we end up laughing together, crying together, praying together, planning together, rejoicing together, dreaming together, working together, or just being together.

LAW #3. COMMITMENT CEMENTS A MARRIAGE SO
THAT IT REMAINS STRONG UNDER TESTING

A trip to the dictionary shows that COMMITMENT means "to give over." Something can be given over for safekeeping, like entrusting the kids to a babysitter. Something also can be given over for whatever purpose the receiver chooses, like dropping a check into the offering basket at church. Either way, a commitment is a hands-off release of our rights over something, which is based on a promise or agreement we make. Human nature drives us to make laws for enforcing certain commitments, like a rental agreement or mortgage. We put ourselves under accountability to an agency, which has the power to enforce our commitment. There are conditional, temporary, and lifelong commitments:

> *Conditional:* "If you keep your pet out of my yard, I will not make a rug out of him for our entryway!"
>
> *Temporary:* "I will join your carpool for one month."
> *Life-long:* "I will be true to you as long as I live."

The best marriages I have seen are built on life-long commitments from both the husband and wife, first to God for accountability, and then to each other for mutual trust.

Broken commitments and heartbreak go together. We had a landlord whose wife became slowly paralyzed with a disease. He filed for divorce while she was in a long term facility. "Until death do us part...(unless you get sick!)"

I also have a friend whose wife is sick with a progressive terminal illness. They are spending whatever days they have left together as he tries to make her comfortable. He told me that it is hard for him to watch her slip, but he will be with her until God takes her home to heaven. Commitment.

Our wedding was a big event in a midwestern, hometown church. Friends, relatives, and people who hardly knew us came. The script included vows to each other, and we stated our commitments to each other in front of a hundred or more people. Ceremony. I doubt if either of us was concentrating on the words at the time! We already had stated our commitments to each other in the most somber way we knew months before. Neither of us knew much about commitment at the time. All we knew was that we wanted a marriage which would last as long as we did.

Since that warm, humid evening in August, we have reaffirmed our commitments as we have discovered more about marriage. Several discoveries, which have deepened our commitments, came from the Bible. First of all, God designed marriage to be a life-long commitment:

> *A man shall leave his father and mother and be joined to his wife, and the two shall become one flesh. (Ephesians 5:31)*

That describes an irreversible process, as God designed it. It's like an ice cube (water) being dropped into boiling water; the two become one, and you don't unscramble them again.

Also, the marriage commitment is a picture of the love of God:

> *Husbands, love your wives, just as Christ also loved the church and gave Himself for it. (Ephesians 5:25)*

Since Christ is the eternal Son of God, His love must also be eternal:

> *For I am persuaded that neither death nor life, nor-angels nor principalities nor powers, nor things present nor things to come nor height nor depth, nor any other created thing, shall be able to separate us from the love of God which is in Christ Jesus our Lord.*
> *(Romans 8:38, 39)*

That tells me that I can love my wife with a love like God has for us, which sounds like the longest commitment conceivable!

I think that our commitment is often measured, not by all the things we WILL do, but by what we WON'T do! With that in mind, I examined my own marriage commitment. As long as our hearts are pumping, I expect us to finish the race together. If that includes the sunset years and our legs still work, we may find ourselves shuffling along with that sack of groceries, and I would attempt to be a gentleman by holding her by the arm. I would still open the door for her. If it so happened, I would sit by her bedside, assuring her that I was still there, even if she didn't recognize me. I would try to be there holding her hand when she was ushered into the arms of Christ in the heavenly place He has gone to prepare. And according to His promises, I would be able to rejoice through my tears that she was with Him...until I went to be with Him, too...where she would be the second one to welcome me home. Of course, our final exit roles might be reversed, but our lifetime commitments to each other are the same.

My dad broke whatever commitment he ever made to my mother. It tells me it can happen. It makes me think seriously about how I can make a commitment that will last for a lifetime, no matter what.

I think I have the answer. Even though it comes under Old Testament Law, here is how God feels about a vow or commitment which is made to Him:

> *If a man vows a vow to the Lord, or swears by an oath to bind himself by some agreement, he shall not break his word; he shall do according to all that proceeds out of his mouth. (Numbers 30:2)*

If I simply made promises to Phyllis, neither she or civil laws have the power to make me keep them. BUT, if I make the promises to God, He requires it of me. My commitment goes something like this...

> "Dear God, you gave her to me to love and care for while we both are alive on earth. I know that she is precious to you because you tell me to love her as you loved your church sacrificially. I commit myself first of all to you so that you can love her through me, and enable me to help her become the woman of God you are making of her. I promise you that I will be the best, most caring husband for her that is possible with you helping me, as long as we live. Don't ever allow me to hurt her. Take away my life first. Thank you."

LAW #4. CULTIVATING LIFTS A MARRIAGE FROM THE HO-HUM LEVEL TO NEW HEIGHTS OF FRUITFULNESS AND FULFILLMENT.

The happiest people I know are either growing in what they can do, or they are tackling something that they have never done before. They may sign up for a class in oil painting, woodworking, flower arranging, astronomy for anyone who can look upward, drama, a foreign language, auto repair, Old Testament Survey, counseling in crisis pregnancy situations, piano, how to start a mom and pop business from your home, real estate, income tax counseling, and.....the list goes on.

They are excited about life. They have high hopes. They have a "plan B" in case "plan A" does not work out. Failure is not in their vocabulary. Their optimism is contagious. Their enthusiasm draws a crowd. People want to be with them.

By contrast, the grumpiest, meanest, most bored-with-life people I know are those who have walled themselves inside their comfort zones. To break out is formidable; the risk is too high. I know some professors who are like that. They teach the same course year after year, but never update their material. They sigh and yawn a lot while teaching it, and so do the students! They have sunk into a rut where their only enjoyment is either bullying students or finding fault with the administration. I overheard one of them say, with unmistakable glee, "Half my class flunked the exam!" What he seemed to be saying is, "I am so miserable that I had to find enjoyment in flunking half my class!"

These observations have led me to conclude that happiness or grumpiness is a choice. Not that we choose emotional responses, but we do make choices which affect our emotions. It is called CULTIVATING. It also can turn a marriage from surviving to thriving.

I had a vegetable garden when I was growing up, which makes me an "authority" on cultivation! To add to my cultivational experience, Phyllis gave me specific instructions on how often to water her plants when she went to visit her folks for a week some years ago. I will not say much about how many plants died, but there were two that got as much water as the rest, and they survived. They looked as good as they did the day she left. She informed me that those plants were plastic!

Cultivation to a gardener means that you find a sunny spot of ground. Then you dig it, pull weeds, plant seeds, water, pull more weeds, and kill harmful bugs. All the while, the seeds grow. Each one already has the built in capacity to become a radish, carrot, ear of corn, or other vegetable when it is put into the right environment. Cultivation in our marriage comes from making an effort to place ourselves into those environments which encourage growth of various kinds. Phyllis and I have signed up for one or two day seminars on counseling, effective listening, and other topics of interest. We participate in small Bible study groups. We go to plays and musical productions. We go places with the over-fifties group in our church, and spend hours visiting with friends. We step outside our comfort zone and submerge ourselves in new endeavors that can cause growth in our marriage. Some things fizzle, and some things we like to repeat.

Some years passed during which we were each involved in segregated things. Phyllis did the women's Bible study, and I taught Sunday School. These segments of our separate lives seldom crossed. I began to pray for something we could work at together. Secretly, I hoped that it would be something where *she would join me* in what I already liked to do. I wanted to stay inside my comfort zone, and have her step outside of hers! It did not work that way.

We had an opportunity to visit the largest church in the world, the Yoido Full Gospel Church in Seoul, Korea, where we learned about "cell groups." A short time later, our church began a cell group program. Couples were needed to host or lead cell groups, where six to twelve people meet regularly for nurturing and growth in their lives! This developed into a work where we both overlapped and submerged ourselves in a joint activity that has gone on for several years. Cultivation.

The cultivation of a marriage is limited only by the imagination. It is the will of God to grow in His work. His desire is that we

> *Be steadfast, immovable, always abounding in the work of the Lord, knowing that your labor is not in vain in the Lord. (I Corinthians 15:58)*

The four principles I have described involve:

CARING
COMMUNICATING
COMMITMENT
CULTIVATING

They have become four guidelines which have turned our marriage from SURVIVING to THRIVING.

To those who may be married, or expect to be someday, I am confident that you can use the guidelines of this chapter for a springboard to some great ideas for your marriage.

CHAPTER 40

EPILOGUE

What an amazing trick! It was high school physics class and Mr. Grant had come into the classroom, carrying a tuning fork in each hand. They were U-shaped pieces of steel used for tuning pianos. He had stepped onto the platform and stood behind the battered table, on which he had demonstrated many strange phenomena during the semester. I watched closely as he clamped the stem of one tuning fork into a holder. Then he paced back and forth and rambled on about how vibrations make sound, and how sound travels through the air, and a lot of other irrelevant stuff (I thought). The tuning fork he still clutched in his hand bobbed up and down in rhythm to his steps. I kept my eyes on it, forcing myself not to blink. I wished that he would stop talking and get on with the show.

Finally with a single, quick movement, Mr. Grant struck the tuning fork on the table. The room was filled with a musical tone like someone hitting a piano key and holding it down. The intensity of the hum began to fade, and Mr. Grant clasped his other hand around the fork, as if he were attempting to smother the sound. But the humming kept on, like the tuning fork refused to die! He even put it into his pocket, but we could still hear it! There was a twinkle in his eye as he faked a puzzled look and examined it carefully. He shut it up in a desk drawer, but the hum lingered! Everyone was wide-eyed, but no one dared to speak, or break the spell by raising his hand to ask what was happening.

Finally, the secret was revealed. Mr. Grant went over to the other tuning fork, lifted it out of its holder by the stem, and quickly walked around the classroom, holding it close to each student's ear. It continued to emit a weak, but distinct hum! The sound from the tuning fork he had struck on the table had excited the same sound in the other fork because they each had something in common: *wavelength*. They were tuned to the same *wavelength*.

That memory of a high school physics class helps me understand one of the basic mechanisms of encouragement common

162

to men. We hear another tell the story of his painful or perplexing experience. It strikes a common *wavelength* in us. We understand what he felt, as his experience brings our own feelings to the surface. And, because of an inborn part of our composition as men, the story is not over until we have a solution. What did he do? What made things get better? How was the problem solved? How can his experience help me add to my "bag of tricks" for facing my own struggles?

I have taken advantage of this encouragement mechanism in writing this book.

I tell what happened.

I tell how I felt.

I tell how it was resolved.

You have probably noticed my belief that God permitted the struggles in my life for a purpose: *so He could show me again and again that He is the answer to every one of life's problems.* I have included many statements from the Bible because they have given me hope in each discouragement, and also strength to go through it with a persuasion that God is great enough to care about my concerns, whether big or small, because He invites us to,

...Cast all your care upon Him, for He cares for you.
(I Peter 5:7)

People who know me realize that I do not pound people on the head with a Bible if they don't believe exactly like I do. Nevertheless, I have come to believe that the Bible has answers, because I am still finding them. But I also recognize that others may not have discovered the message of hope offered on the pages of the Bible. If the Bible has not directly influenced your life for good with the hope it offers, it may be for several reasons:

— you have never gotten around to reading the Bible;
— you may have lived with an opinion that the Bible is incorrect, inaccurate, or irrelevant, and do not want to take time to examine it;
— you may be content in whatever you believe now, and have no compelling desire to search elsewhere.

If any of these reasons describes your view, I want to close this book by offering the greatest possible encouragement I know: I encourage you to boldly test the Bible. Read it. Not all at once. A few verses or chapters each day. If the Bible is truth, as it claims, and if the ultimate source of it is God himself, as it claims, you might sense a response inside—like the tuning fork. You may even sense that the Author knows you personally! No one needs to be there to give you their slant on what you are reading, or tell you what you should believe about it. Test it yourself. Give it a chance to prove itself to you.

ABOUT THE AUTHOR

Dr. Fred Moody is an engineer who did undergraduate work at the University of Colorado, and graduate work at Stanford. He has worked over 38 years at General Electric in San Jose, California, analyzing energy system behavior under adverse conditions, with major emphasis on nuclear safety and containment. He teaches advanced engineering courses to practicing engineers, and has been an adjunct professor at San Jose State University since 1971. He has written over 50 technical papers, an engineering textbook, and co-authored several other books on engineering. He has given technical seminars in the U. S., Europe, Asia, and the Middle East. Dr. Moody is a Christian as described in Bible verses like John 3:16, Romans 3:23, and I Corinthians 15:3, 4. He and Phyllis, his wife of 41 years, have four grown sons, two daughters-in-law, and six grandchildren.